PENGUIN BOOKS
Ciao Tuscany

Ciao Tuscany

Allan Parker

PENGUIN BOOKS

PENGUIN BOOKS

Penguin Books (NZ) Ltd, cnr Airborne and Rosedale Roads, Albany,
Auckland 1310, New Zealand
Penguin Books Ltd, 27 Wrights Lane, London W8 5TZ, England
Penguin Putnam Inc, 375 Hudson Street, New York, NY 10014, United States
Penguin Books Australia Ltd, 487 Maroondah Highway, Ringwood,
Australia 3134
Penguin Books Canada Ltd, 10 Alcorn Avenue, Toronto, Ontario,
Canada M4V 3B2
Penguin Books (South Africa) Pty Ltd, 5 Watkins Street, Denver Ext 4, 2094,
South Africa
Penguin Books India (P) Ltd, 11, Community Centre, Panchsheel Park,
New Delhi 110 017, India

Penguin Books Ltd, Registered Offices: Harmondsworth, Middlesex, England

First published by Penguin Books (NZ) Ltd, 2001

3 5 7 9 10 8 6 4 2

Copyright © Allan Parker, 2001

The right of Allan Parker to be identified as the author of this work in terms of
section 96 of the Copyright Act 1994 is hereby asserted.

Editorial services by Michael Gifkins & Associates
Designed by Mary Egan
Typeset by Egan-Reid Ltd
Printed in Australia by McPhersons Printing Group

ISBN 0 14 100558 0

Contents

This book is dedicated to the memory of two good people.

To Dave: fine friend and unwitting matchmaker.
Sadly, I could not show him Tuscany and my new life.

To Hannalore: an eternal beacon of happiness and
warmth who befriended a stranger in paradise.

*It is also for my new Americans. They applaud endeavour,
don't scorn it. They encourage effort, do not ignore it.
They nourish poppies, not worrying about their height.*

*It's also for the friends we made in Tuscany,
the welcome we had from Civetta
and the warmth of all Tuscans.*

*And, as it will always be, it's for Nancy—
friend, lover, soul-mate, valued critic,
exceptional and uncomplaining typist.*

Prima Parte

L'apertura

We are very lucky.
We grow in a beautiful place.

—*Barone Francesco Ricasoli*,
32ND BARON OF CASTELLO DI BROLIO,
RADDA IN CHIANTI, TUSCANY

One

Renato, the true Tuscan from Rome

WITH only two days left in Tuscany I met my first true rural Tuscan. For three years I had lived in the isolated 300-year-old villa San Clemente outside the little village of Trequanda. For the last two, my new wife Nancy had shared the serenity. Yet in all that time, we had never encountered someone who so perfectly represented the way of life in this area. Elario, the former peasant farmer who grew up at San Clemente, had been the closest—but he came from a dead era, the 400-year *mezzadria*, or share-cropping, system that died out after World War Two.

Renato was today's true Tuscan, a small, independent farmer at peace and in harmony with his world. And he was not even Tuscan. In fact, he looked as if the winter winds of Siberia had swept him here straight from the Russian steppes. The large land-holdings around San Clemente and its village across the hills, Trequanda of the distant pension fund Cariplo, no more represented the Tuscan vitality than the chic fashion houses on

Florence's Via de' Tornabuoni. But, to me, Renato was Tuscan to the bone of one of his home-cured prosciuttos.

It was early evening, about 6 p.m., as Lassi the Finn and I drove through the small village of Pozzo della Chiana and down the hill on the other side of town towards Lucignano. We were going to refill Lassi's empty flagons with more of Renato's wine.

At the bottom of the hill, a left turn. Another left about five or six hundred metres further along, but this time onto a summer-dusty dirt drive up to the Baroncini family home. We were lucky to find space to park in the front yard among the dogs and cats and chickens, the litter of farm tools, the cluster of sheds and assorted vehicles.

The whole family came out at the commotion we set up among the roaming animals.

First, Renato, the undisputed king of his domain. He was a squat, powerfully built man with a ruddy face that might have been burnt by the snow blizzards of the steppes as much as by the scorching heat of the summer sun at this time of year. At sixty-one years, he was as healthy as a glass of his wine and as strong as the pickles in his jars. His thickly muscled arms poured from the short sleeves of his white T-shirt, rather than poked meekly out of them. His forearm muscles were as hard as day-old saltless Tuscan bread; they could break a stack of terracotta roof tiles just by threatening them. As he stood by the doorway in his blue work dungarees, here at a first glance was not just a Tuscan man but Tuscany itself.

Beside him, her typically Tuscan red hair framing a welcoming face, was Adelaide, his wife for thirty-six years. Together, they produced three children. One, Roberto the bricklayer, still lives at home with his wife Angelita and their thirteen-year-old son Andrea.

Lassi had seemed a little nervous about taking me with him on his wine-replenishment mission. 'You're the first *straniero*, foreigner, I've brought here except for Finns.' Lassi, the ex-drummer in a gold-disc-winning dance band, and his wife Paivi moved to Tuscany six months after I arrived. They leased a small holiday home complex clustered around an inviting pool. The attractions of Tuscany—warmth, beauty, history, food, wine—means they only have to advertise in Finland for business. The move was a leap of faith, but one that has paid off for them. But he needn't have worried about unleashing a Kiwi on the Baroncini family.

'Ah, *Luna Rossa* (Red Moon),' announced Renato as Lassi introduced me as his New Zealand friend. The reference was to the recent America's Cup contest against the New Zealand holder and its *Black Magic* yacht. The Italians followed the finals with keen interest, particularly in Tuscany, home of the team's leader and *Luna Rossa*'s official yacht club. For many months after the finals, the words *Luna Rossa* were invariably uttered when people discovered I was from New Zealand. But despite the 5–0 drubbing by *Black Magic*, there was never a note of lament at such a comprehensive loss, more a pride that it was Italy who beat the other challengers to reach the finals. I always tried to be diplomatic by saying it would have been better as 5–4, a one-point winning margin in the best-of-nine finals. As long as it was New Zealand with the five points, mind you! This response was always greeted with good spirits.

So with the shared knowledge of *Luna Rossa* glowing warmly between us, we crossed the threshold into the house that Renato and Adelaide have made their home for thirty years. He was born and raised in a village called Pavona Di Albano Laziale, then about twenty-five kilometres south of Rome. In 1939, his father planted his vines 'and also me'. But papa died just ten months after that seed he planted was born as Renato.

As he grew older, he too 'started to work with the vine'. He eventually became quite famous locally for his red wine. He also worked in a bakery and, for quite a time, as a *camionista*, a truck driver for a laundry.

His first sight of Tuscany was on a train ride through it during his compulsory military service. He fell in love with its beauty and a new seed was planted—to return one day and buy a small vineyard or farm atop a Tuscan hill. That's what Tuscany does to you—the Finns, our German friends, Renato . . . it is like a visual drug when you first see its beauty; you have to come back for another fix.

Throughout these years, he continued to live at home. But as the youngest of three, he was the least important on the Italian family rating scale. The eldest was always *Numero Uno*. Still, after he and Adelaide married, the new couple moved in to share the house with his mother and the elder brother (the middle sibling, his sister, had presumably married and left to live with her husband). 'It was a disaster,' he recalls of those immediate post-wedding years.

Worse, the older brother began secretly stealing Renato's now highly prized wine and selling it himself. When Renato found out there was little he could do except, when he had the money, buy a small place of his own nearby for his vines.

If trouble was brewing at home, it was also marching south from over the northern horizon. The village was expanding, with workers from the Eternal City needing cheap and available housing; year by year, the city itself was moving nearer, a monstrous urban whale devouring countryside, hamlets, farms and villages like Renato's as it wallowed over the landscape. 'Too much people, cars, hurry, pollution, less friendly people—including brother and mother.' It was the eternal conflict of progress and traditional lifestyles.

Finally enough was enough for Renato. He quietly travelled back to Tuscany and bought his little farm between Pozzo and Lucignano. A few months later, he and Adelaide left with the two young children they had by then produced.

They told no one where they were going, not even mama and the despised older brother. His first task on his new farm was to plant two hectares in vines, then get work outside the farm as a wood-cutter to earn a living while waiting for the vines to grow.

Today, his little enterprise has expanded to ten hectares. Eight are his own and he leases another two from the neighbours. He mostly works only his own land, alone during the week and with son Roberto beside him on weekends. Sometimes he helps local people by pruning their olive trees, vines, garden trees and the like.

At the time we met he had only one hectare planted in vines, about 2500 plants. Ten years ago, when the market price of wine was higher, he had more than 10,000 plants, producing 60,000–70,000 litres of excellent eleven per cent alcohol wine. Today's one hectare produces 5000 litres, still of excellent quality, but with thirteen per cent alcohol. Between them, Renato and Roberto drink about 2000 of those litres each year—an average of nearly 5.5 litres a day. That may sound a lot, but in Italy it doesn't raise an eyebrow.

The balance of the wine he sells only to Lassi and to a man from Milan; although other people would like to buy it he simply says there is no wine to sell.

The only chemical he uses anywhere on his farm is a dilute potassium bisulphate. When the grapes start to ferment, they would easily turn into vinegar without this. But for the plants he does not use chemicals or fertilisers, just manure from his animals. Apart from the vines, he grows wheat, corn and barley.

He raises about twelve cows a year, selling the meat to the local butcher shops (about 3000 kilos a year). The price is going up all the time because his cows are organically raised and there is no risk of the Mucca Pazza (Mad Cow Disease). He raises pigs, about two to four a year. Like the wine, they are only for his family and selected friends like Lassi. He buys the pigs, prepares the hams and makes the salamis and sausages. Of the hams, the family eats up to six a year. The rest he sells to friends. He charges them 25,000 lire a kilo for the *prosciutto crudo*, the air-cured hams.

As we all sat at the big wooden table dominating the centre of the room that acts as kitchen, dining room, family room and social centre, he told me how he makes his cured hams.

The prized *prosciutto crudo* is made from the shoulder of the pig.

'You massage *sale grosso* (rock salt) into the meat and leave for one day per kilo. Each day bend the bone a little.' After, say, twenty-five days, cover the ham with minced *peperoncini*, chili peppers ('but not hot'). A big woven basket piled high with the little *peperoncini* sat on the gleaming dark-wood sideboard behind him, waiting for the next prosciutto.

Then you hang the prosciutto for two years at a constant temperature, 18–25 degrees Celsius. At that stage, you test it for freshness. This is done by smell. A knitting needle made of horse cartilage is plunged into the centre of the ham and, depending on the smell of the meat in the centre, Renato can tell whether the prosciutto is 'done' or needs more curing. The horse cartilage is used because it does not absorb the *profumo*, the perfume, of the ham; it just carries it, so it can be cleaned and constantly re-used as fresh and untainted.

I had already seen this at Enrico's, our local Trequanda butcher. He was quite famed for the quality of his meats and two men in business suits had come to buy stocks of his *bistecca* (the giant T-bone steaks of the Chianina cattle used to make *bistecca Fiorentina*), salami, sausages—and a *prosciutto crudo*.

It was a serious, solemn, even religious process. Enrico carefully laid the ham on top of his glass-faced counter. He produced his 'needle' and dug it deep into the ham. Withdrawing it, he slowly sniffed the aroma he had obtained, then passed the needle to the two 'suits'. There was a lively discussion, then Enrico repeated the process. More discussion. It was all very serious. And who can blame them—at 25,000 lire a kilo, a twenty-five kilo prosciutto is worth 625,000 lire. But everything seemed satisfactory and Enrico took the prosciutto into the preparation room behind the shop to vacuum-pack it for travel.

The thing with the smell is obviously like the 'nose' of a wine to the vintner. Only training and experience will give you the ability to check the 'rightness' of the ham. A mistake is a costly one in terms of effort, time and eating pleasure.

All this time, Renato had been standing at the table carving wafer-thin slices from one of his prosciutto on a wooden carving board. The slices were passed around on a plate for us to take and eat with thick slices of fresh bread. To wash it down, we had glasses of his velvet-smooth, glorious red wine. His reputation was certainly justified. We poured the wine from one-litre plastic water and Coke bottles. It's a common enough practice for wine-makers to 'recycle' these as wine bottles.

Now it was time to fill those flagons of Lassi's and we were led into a room off the family room.

'This is my church,' said Renato as he entered the room.

He was wrong. For *any* Tuscan, this short, narrow, dimly-lit room was like heaven.

Lining each side were tall benches. On one of these sat two, two thousand-litre vats of Renato's wine; another sat on the other side. Ageing prosciutto hams dangled from hooks hanging down from the exposed rafters. Bunches of cherry tomatoes were draped over the rafters; kept in this environment they will stay fresh for many months. Big jars of mixed pickles, each a multi-coloured piece of nature's art, sat on the benches around the vats—small onions, peppers, artichokes, chili peppers, carrots. The room itself was starkly bare, practical. Who needed pretty paintwork or fancy woodwork when these family jewels provided all the atmosphere?

How marvellously self-sufficient Renato and his family were. And with the warmth of welcome and joy in all their eyes evident, how at peace they were with themselves and their existence.

They did not need more land, did not have a drive to expand, to make more money, to exploit the fields beyond recovery.

It is a Tuscan way of life, one he enjoys and feels part of. His days as a Roman are long gone and when he does go to the Eternal City he finds himself wanting to return to his own land within half a day—'too much traffic, noise, pollution and aggressive people'.

Here, on his eight hectares, he appreciates the clean air to breath and natural, biological food to eat.

'The harmony of the people and nature still exists. People are friendly, honest and modest. Hard work is still appreciated as a virtue.

'I love to work in the beautiful landscape, the simple way of living, the visits each day to the (Bar) Circolo at Pozzo, the freedom of being my own boss, the friendliness of the people of Pozzo.'

He knows the townsfolk still regard him as Roman. But that is typical for any outsider coming to a small rural community; it takes generations to be fully accepted as 'one of us'. And it would only make matters worse to fight it.

So Renato has accepted it. And the town has accepted him. 'He is considered a friend of everybody,' said Lassi. Finally, Tuscany means freedom and independence from his not-so-happy younger years and the stresses of city life.

If there is one word to describe Renato's way of life it is . . . balance. It's a word Nancy used to describe the lifestyle that gives Tuscans their special qualities of openness, warmth, joy, laughter and honesty.

'They have a balance of life between work, family, friends and fun,' she said.

He works hard. He spends time with his family, he has his friends and he enjoys his daily visit to the Bar Circolo. He makes sure he has time for all.

This well-rounded life is the formula of the Tuscans. There is always time for everything: the kids may go cycling, mum and dad may take a hike or an after-dinner stroll in the town, the grandfolk like to meet for a chat in the piazzas.

And if they are in harmony with themselves, so too are they in harmony with nature. Their window boxes and gardens are rainbows in summer, the little garden plots are tended and protected as carefully as the young grandchildren, the walks in the woods provide fresh herbs, mushrooms, chestnuts, berries . . . they take only what they need.

And that's the secret—be happy, be balanced, be content with what you have, be a Tuscan. It took us three years to find it. But the journey was always a memorable one.

Seconda Parte

Things to do

Chi ha pochi desideri é ricco.
Who has few desires is rich.

—Tuscan proverb

Two

Entering the new millennium

AS spring begins again at our villa, San Clemente on the slopes above the Valdichiana, sex-crazed owls play havoc with our sleep.

First, an owl emerges from wherever it is that owls go for winter to set up residence on the closest branch of the acacia tree it can find outside our bedroom window.

It is a screech owl. Naturally!

As the warming weather fires up its mating lust, it becomes increasingly raucous.

Finally it finds a mate—and we have to endure an hours-long screech owl sexual frenzy. Their big night begins with soft whisperings which I presume is the equivalent of foreplay. Then they build to a screaming crescendo that includes much flapping of wings.

They take a breather for twenty or so minutes and then are at it again. This all starts about 2 a.m. It doesn't stop until first light, when they seem to be sated and head off for a day of rest.

I feel like a voyeur at an orgy. As I try to get a couple of hours' sleep, I can only hope that their night of passion has done the trick; another night of screech owl sex would be unbearable.

At least with the appearance of the owls, we know that spring is on the way and we can look forward to six or seven months of warm weather.

Actually this past winter has not been as hard as the first two. We had two light snowfalls. The one in December was just a light overnight dusting that quickly melted from the countryside. The second, in January, was a little heavier and snow along the shaded roadside banks and in the woods lingered for some days. But it quickly disappeared from our dirt lane.

This was a blessing. The Italian authorities have an extremely efficient snow and ice clearing system for all public roads. I guess this is because of the country's obsession with cars. But our lane is a *strada privata*, a private road, and they feel no obligation to keep it clear. The previous winter, Nancy's first here, we had a hefty dump. As we drove back and forth on shopping expeditions, the snow turned to thick pack ice. In places it was, perhaps, an inch thick. The worst was on the corner at the top where there is a steep drop towards the even steeper bank on the side, above the field. Here, the jeep threatened to slide down and over the bank before the four-wheel drive took charge. It was an unpleasant, frightening stretch of the lane to cross.

The villa was still cold but we had the pre-winter foresight to stockpile wood for the big open fireplace in the lounge. We borrowed a chainsaw from Joe the German in Petroio. Some of the timber came from dead trees and limbs in the woods. But the bulk was right on hand, neatly stacked in our courtyard—massive roof beams, as much as a half-metre square.

For centuries they supported the heavy tiles above the animal and equipment storage sheds across the courtyard from the main house. Time, neglect, woodworms, climate and rot eventually conspired against them and the whole central section of the roof collapsed; it must have been a fearsome noise, the thud of the heavy beams mingled with the clatter of the roof tiles they brought down with them. A month or so ago, some workmen looking for a leak in the water pipe to Miciano, the old monastery that is now split into holiday apartments further down the lane, stopped to ask if we knew where the underground pipe ran; I had no idea. The obvious head of the threesome so admired the villa that I invited them in to have a look.

'*Bella, bella,*' he mutters as we tour the downstairs. 'Beautiful, beautiful.' This is the reaction of most who come into the villa despite its bare walls and sparse furnishings.

Before he leaves on his water leak search, he points to the beams in the kitchen and the formal dining room. These are original, he says knowledgeably. The ones in the lounge are not, probably installed at the time the house was renovated some time in the last twenty or so years.

As I sit here now at the kitchen table writing, I cast an anxious eye at the beams above me. They seem to have taken on a menacing air. What mischief have the woodworms done, how much dry rot has worked through them, I wonder. How safe are they?

Someone cleared away the rubble of tiles and neatly stacked the beams against the still-standing wall that separated the sheds from the peasant family's outside bakehouse. Or rather, an army of men. Each beam is murderously heavy, too much for one, two, even four people to heft up on to the growing pile.

I had no qualms about sawing them up for firewood. Once majestic, they are now just sorry reminders of the days of the *mezzadria*, when a peasant family filled the villa with themselves and their animals. The woodworms still do their work as does the dry rot. The beams will never be used again and it would be an expensive business to have them trucked away.

Another, unexpected source of wood also arrived in time for winter. The telephone people decided to replace all the poles down the lane. The old ones, rotted at the base, they abandoned on the side of the lane and we asked if we could help ourselves. '*Non problema.*' One of the workmen must have told his family because first thing the next morning, mamma and papa turned up in their little three-wheeler Ape (*ah-pay*), parked outside our place, began chainsawing the poles and loading up the tray. We sprang into action and collected as many as we could, towing them back behind the jeep. We managed to collect about fifteen, dumping each load on the front lawn. We would worry about cutting them up later.

The poles are filled with ants' nests. But our need was greater than theirs and they and their home faced a fiery future.

The wood from the forest, the beams and the poles filled the one shed that retains its roof (that too could collapse at any time; one beam was rotted away so much in a corner that it had to be propped up) and spills over to the outside wall of the shed.

Throughout December and January, the fire brought welcome additional warmth into the lounge and spread cheer throughout the downstairs. The heat from the flames also filtered up through the tiled ceiling and took the chill off the upstairs bedrooms and library. By raising the grate on bricks to bring the fire closer to the chimney, we also removed the problem of smoke in the house that we had the previous winter. But an open fire is a voracious one and the stockpile quickly dwindled, so much so that the wood lasted only two of the three winter months we had hoped to get from it.

At least we had enough for our Christmas Day dinner. We decided to invite friends for a mid-afternoon meal with all the trimmings.

Our guest list was an international cast—Italy, England, Germany, Finland, and of course us, representing New Zealand and the United States. The names reflected the nationalities: Rosalbo (Italy), Laura (England), Hannalore and Reiner (Germany), Lassi, Paivi, Heli, Paavo and Kaarina (Finland), Allan (New Zealand) and Nancy (USA). You will meet most of the guests again as our life in Tuscany unfolds.

Both of us enjoy the spirit of Christmas and in the lead-up to the event, we selected a tree from the woods, a juniper with fiercely sharp needles that bit into your fingers and arms. We set it up where the foyer runs into the lounge. Then we decorated it to the sound of Christmas music. We strung fairy lights through the tree and placed handmade origami stars, floating swans and flying cranes among the branches. I sprinkled cotton wool balls around the tree to imitate snow. Nancy gathered pine cones and branches with their dead leaves still on them. Then she spray-painted them with gold and silver and spread them around the room and in the tree branches.

It was simple but effective. There is something rather nice about our do-it-yourself Christmas decorating. Anyway, we didn't want to spend money on 'professional' decorations. We have no permanent need for them and they would merely be a nuisance when we decided to move on.

Our menu had an international flavour to it as well. We started with steaming mulled wine (an English recipe, although our German and Finnish friends have their own recipes for mulled wine) then made *bruschetta* (Italy) over the coals in the fireplace—thick slices of bread toasted crisp on the outside but still soft in the middle, then rubbed on both sides with freshly halved garlic cloves, sprinkled with a little salt and then finally drenched with the new season's olive oil, from the harvest just a month before. The newly pressed olive oil adds a sharp, hot tang; over the months it loses this bite but for now it is a glorious taste. Rosalbo quickly stepped in to help. This was, after all, typical fare of his native Tuscany and he had no intention of letting some dumb Kiwi get it wrong.

Then we moved to the dining room. The main course was roast turkey with cranberry sauce and the trimmings like stuffing, gravy, potatoes and pumpkin. This was Nancy's contribution to the menu. The Germans brought a salad to follow the turkey. Laura provided the English dessert—a hot, steamed Christmas pudding, rich and dark with brandy cream sauce which she served *flambé*. She brought it back from an early December visit to England. With New Zealand's English heritage I was quite familiar with a Christmas pudding. But it was a complete novelty to all the others, who had never seen or tasted one before. Many went back for seconds.

The Finns completed it all with bitter-sweet, dark chocolate Paivi's parents had brought with them for their month-long holiday escape in Tuscany. Who can blame them for wanting to escape the Finnish winter; the town they live in about half way between the southern capital Helsinki and the northern border gets minus 40 degrees Celsius temperatures in those dark months, even colder when the winds blow. Tuscany, even in winter, must seem like a tropical paradise to them.

The wine and laughter flowed easily, as did the after-dinner liqueurs as we moved back into the lounge where I played Father Christmas. We had bought everyone an inexpensive little fun gift. Rosalbo, for example, is a determined Gemini so we found a horoscope book for the coming millennium year. Hannalore and Reiner were about to begin cleaning up their new house which promised to be a messy, dusty job; for them we had a little plastic dust pan and brush and a next-to-useless set of screwdrivers. And so on.

Then the CDs, tapes and albums got the partying under way. Unfortunately no one volunteered to play the grand piano. Lassi, having been a drummer in Finland, will on occasion play a song or two but he hasn't the formal training. Hannalore, who studied piano as a young girl from a teacher who was as interested in correct posture as the sounds she made, didn't feel comfortable entertaining us after not playing for years. Stan, our American friend from Long Island, is one of the few visitors we had who would sit at the piano with confidence even though he can't read a note. However he can play any tune that someone can hum or sing.

Still, we had plenty of recorded music on hand to satisfy us. We could offer jazz, blues, classical, the Boss, opera, relics from the Sixties (like myself), Latin, hard rock, gentle rock, country rock, even Elvis singing Christmas carols.

At first the music gravitated towards classical refrains as the women gracefully waltzed around the lounge occasionally touching outreached palms for a bit of a twirl.

As the Christmas spirit continued to flow, people became bolder about making their own selection. Even Paivi's parents got into the act. It's an undecided vote on who provided the evening's highlight—Paivi's father conducting Verdi with a firewood branch, her mother bursting into a deep-voiced aria or your author standing on the piano chair and stripping (to the waist only!) to Ravel's *Bolero*. Torvill and Dean, I thought at the time, would have been proud of me. In the sober light of the next day, I knew otherwise.

On these high and low notes, the party wound down. We had timed the Christmas dinner to start at four p.m. so that by the time the after-dinner frolics were overtaken by the tiredness of the day and the effects of the food, alcohol and partying, everyone could get home at a reasonable hour.

The way Italians celebrate Christmas is rather different. Their Christmas period starts, literally and religiously, on 8 December each year (*Immacolata Concezione*), when lights in each town come on, trees go up in homes and stores begin their relentless sales drives. This last Christmas we did notice some more aggressive retailers began their pitches earlier. The Italian Christmas Day actually begins on Christmas Eve. The family gathers for Christmas dinner of fish and shellfish which may start at say 8 p.m. Afterwards, it is time for the opening of presents. Then the family head out to Midnight Mass or the disco or both, as one young Italian explained it to me. While Mum and Dad will then return home, the young folk get back home about 5 a.m. to crash until early Christmas Day afternoon when it's time for another big family meal.

By then, I would imagine, everyone has had enough of Christmas until next year. But the trees and lights will remain in place, again religiously, until 7 January (*Epifania*). Italian superstition holds that it is bad luck not to remove the decorations on that day.

I am not a churchgoer, but I do like the traditional midnight Christmas choral service. Hannalore and Reiner said they had been to an excellent one in the beautiful abbey of Monte Oliveto Maggiore, perhaps a twenty-minute drive, the previous Christmas Eve. So on Nancy's first Christmas, we four decided to go. It was excruciating.

We walked into a full-blown Mass: bishop, monks, interminable chanting, no audience participation, no carols. Nancy and I left after one and a half hours, when the cheap plastic doll 'representing' Baby Jesus was presented to the altar. Reiner said later that the show went on for another thirty minutes with more of the same. But the place was packed—standing room only, and most of that taken.

If Christmas Day was a rowdy affair, our millennium New Year was tame by comparison. We decided to stay at San Clemente, just the two of us.

About 11.15 p.m., we heated some of the mulled wine still left from the previous week, put it into vacuum flasks and, thus armed with fortifying warmth, drove down to Miciano, the apartment block down the dirt lane.

Most towns and villages, at least around us, always have a New Year fireworks display as midnight falls. Because the towns are so small, these are generally pretty modest affairs. But they do acknowledge the passing of hopes and dreams for the future. Even the smallest of towns puts on some sort of display.

We felt sure that the uniqueness of the passage of a thousand years would prompt each community to rise to the occasion with a grander-than-usual effort.

And so it proved.

We sat in the dark on the low wall of the terrace at the back of the old monastery that itself may have seen the passing of ten centuries. We used a torch to fill glasses with the hot wine. It was, fortunately, quite a mild night for that time of year so our coats, gloves and spicy hot drinks kept any chill at bay.

We knew when we entered the twenty-first century because the apartment above us broke into cheers and applause; the occupants had obviously been watching the countdown on television. They had arrived a day or so before but we had never met them. I think they must have borrowed the apartment from the parents of one of the group.

Within seconds the Valdichiana spread out below us erupted with exploding star shells and soaring rockets as this part of Tuscany celebrated. It was certainly obvious that every town, village and hamlet was taking their fun seriously. There must have been fifty or more separate displays performing for us sitting high in the Gods above the valley floor. To the north, we could see as far as Monte San Savino; to the south, Montepulciano's big night was masked by the ridgeline across from us. Away in the hills on the other side of the valley, Cortona was surrounded by the exploding fireworks in the sky above it. But most impressive was Sinalunga, fortunately the closest to us—about three kilometres in a straight line—so we got the sound effects from the bigger star shells, the noise reaching us a few seconds after the actual detonation.

Even restaurants and individual homes got into the celebratory mood. Many local restaurants had advertised a New Year's Eve dinner with a display at midnight. The fish restaurant, Le Logge, down the hill a little and across a gully, perhaps five hundred metres in a straight line but a six kilometre drive away, put on its own show—and a quite impressive one at that—for its clientele and us. Further down, a farmhouse set off skyrockets and other fireworks.

I later estimated that our grandstand view encompassed about a thousand square kilometres—not bad for a free fireworks display!

Although it was the two of us sitting there in the dark, we didn't feel at all isolated or lonely. Tuscany was not that bad a place to be bringing in a new millennium.

In this way we entered the year 2000. But it was only a little later, with the promise of spring, that I felt our new year was starting. For me there would be two milestones. In April, I would reach my half-century. Then, a week later, *Seasons in Tuscany* would be published, the book that covered my first year at San

Clemente and meeting and marrying Nancy.

The time since then had been a continuing discovery of the richness of life at San Clemente, in Tuscany and even further afield. There was to be familiarity and surprises. And the summer ahead . . .

Three

A day in the hills of Tuscany

'IF you're going to get into this tourist business, Allan, the first thing you've got to know is where the dunnies are,' said Neil, the hard-bitten but eminently practical Aussie. It was good advice.

In time I went into the tour guide business. It was a modest little venture. There were motives. It gave me a day away from the isolation of San Clemente. It provided a chance to meet new people from around the world. It gave me beer, wine and cigarette pocket money. And I genuinely enjoyed sharing the beauty of Tuscany with newcomers. The tours were an outgrowth of the day tour I took Nancy on during her first visit and then other house guests who came to stay.

The 'Day in the hills of Tuscany' was a relative success given its limitations, self-imposed or necessary. The main self-imposed limitation was to do the tour just one day a week since I was also writing *Seasons in Tuscany*, which was a consuming effort physically and, more draining, mentally. I chose a Monday on the premise that most foreign tourists from, say, England and America, arrived on a weekend and might appreciate some early orientation and sightseeing. It had to show key elements of the rural Tuscan lifestyle and landscape. It could not be too arduous—plenty of time for stops and walk-arounds.

The necessary limitations were imposed by legal and bureaucratic constraints.

Italy is essentially a police state. I lost track of the number of police forces the country manages to field; *carabinieri*, municipal, provincial, railway, forest . . . the list is seemingly endless. Most seem to be job creation programmes, their personnel unnecessary otherwise. Apart from the omnipotent paramilitary *carabinieri*, the tax police are the most feared.

It's a ludicrous situation: the State taxes people heavily only to pay it back in pensions and healthcare and so on (no doubt with corruption and graft on the side). But because the tax is so high, there is a vigorous black economy, particularly among the tradespeople. So to counter this, there is an equally vigorous—and large—corps of tax police. Licensed businesses like shops, restaurants and services are terrified of them; they insist that you take your printout receipt from the cash register as you get your purchases. These are proof, if you are stopped by the tax police, that you have made a legitimate purchase and the shop has the legitimate documentation in its internal accounting system. One shopkeeper even ran down the street after us because we forgot the receipt. Yet ironically, in the three years that I lived in Italy I was never once stopped by the tax police and never knew anyone else who was.

It seems so obvious: overtax the people and they'll try to hide it, bring it to a reasonable level and they will be more willing to see the benefits—and pay. One estimate I read noted that some forty per cent of the Italian economy was 'black', 'cash', 'under the table', whatever you like to call it. That's an astounding percentage of the national economy.

But necessarily I had to become part of that black economy for my little day excursions, the simple reason being that I was not registered to work in Italy. I had to avoid being noticed by the tax police and keep a low profile by promoting the tours only with *stranieri*, foreign friends who rented holiday apartments to tourists from outside Italy. I felt no guilt about it—I was injecting foreign money into the economy through van rentals, lunches, café stops, petrol. But I still knew I had to keep my head down.

I never wanted it to become a huge success, either in volume or income. I had thought initially to provide the service to the holiday apartment rental places around Trequanda. But thinking it through, even that was too risky—the *carabinieri* in the town knew everyone's affairs, talked to and recognised everyone. So in the end I decided to ask two resident *stranieri* friends to help promote it by placing a brochure in the apartments they rented to foreign tourists. At least this way there would be no direct Italian involvement.

And that's how it stayed during the rest of our time in Tuscany. Most weeks I had only the one, Monday tour. On rare occasions I would be asked to do an extra mid-week one. Often there were none. They were always in the 'season', May to October. The tourist industry, like the peasants of Tuscany, went into winter hibernation, although Lassi and Paivi got business over the Christmas–New Year period, presumably because even mid-winter Tuscany was a damned sight warmer than Finland. I guess if you're Finnish anywhere is warmer except, perhaps, for the permafrost of Siberia.

I planned the itinerary and then drove over it to see if it was feasible in a day and within the free kilometres allowed before the rental company began charging for each extra one. I wrote and produced a little brochure and made photocopies on garish yellow card; I could not afford a glossy printed production with the tempting photos needed to grab the eye of potential clients.

I was open for business.

The first call one Sunday evening was still a surprise, albeit a pleasant one. It was Neil, the Aussie who was to give me that early piece of advice. His party of four (the largest I ever had was six) wanted to go the next day. It was a nervy night. But I had confidence in the package I had put together. I could talk about the history and the landscape, helped by the research for my first book. It was the style I was more nervous about. I did not want to fling an endless list of names and dates at people, which would promptly be forgotten. Rather, my aim was to let them absorb some of the beauties of this part of Tuscany, images that would be lasting, and at the same time talk a little about Tuscan and Italian customs. By then, I thought I had observed enough to give them some insights without professing to be an expert.

Thus, at 9.30 the next morning outside the Bar L'Angolo in Sinalunga's old-town Piazza Garibaldi, my 'Days in the Hills of Tuscany' began. The bar became the usual pick-up point and I never had any trouble identifying my charges for the day—tourists look alike anywhere.

First was the drive to Trequanda ('this is my village'), then down the hill on the road to Asciano and, further on, towards Siena. This was the edge of Le Crete, the bare 'badlands of Siena'. Away to the right, as stark on its hill as the cypress trees that bring relief to the skyline of this countryside, is the castle of Gallico. Its five towers stand as guardians as they have for seven hundred years since the still-important Tolomei family bought and enlarged its already existing single-towered complex in 1319. It is actually a fortified farm, one of the many in the hills and plains of this territory, and was once an outpost of the territory's rulers to warn against invaders and a protective retreat for the peasants who farmed the surrounding fields. In the first half of the 1400s, a rich silk merchant family from Montepulciano, some thirty kilometres to the south, bought it. Its strategic value was such that the Republic of Siena ordered the family to post a company of soldiers for defence. Over the centuries it has changed hands often. Today, relatively new owners have restored and fenced it so, sadly, our view could only be from a distance.

On the high ridgeline that we would climb to after passing this distant reminder of the centuries of history there is a spectacular view across Le Crete towards Asciano, a dozen or so kilometres to the north. Eroded gullies, rolling and bare hills, isolated farmhouses (most hundreds of years old) and those slender green fingers of the solitary cypresses seeming to reach for life in the deep blue skies of Tuscany; it was always an impressive and imposing sight for my guests as we stopped to admire it. We would not turn right at the T-junction a hundred metres on, but left. We were not going to Asciano or Siena but to one of the most startlingly beautiful sites and sights in Tuscany.

On its narrow ridgeline jutting out from the main road to the Val d'Asso, the brown-bricked monastery of Monte Oliveto Maggiore stands out proudly like a figurehead on an old sailing vessel. On three sides, steep cliffs fall sharply away, deeply etched by the erosion that plagues Le Crete. Dark green, brooding cypresses vie for the space on the narrow, short ridge. The high peaks of the main gateway's square watchtower and, below, the spired top of the Abbey's tower poke beautifully from the cypresses that surround the whole setting.

For seven hundred years, men with strong faith have endured the isolation, the hardship, but also the beauty of the location.

In winter, the drive up through the cypresses to the gateway is almost a religious experience. Snow carpets the forest floor or sits heavily on the bending branches. Swirling white mist gives an ethereal edge to the scene. Here and there, the winter sun finds holes in the mist and the snow sparkles with its rays. There are no hordes of tourists or sounds of turning tour coaches. It is deeply silent.

It is an extraordinarily serene atmosphere, although I do not envy the few monks who live and pray here during the damp and chill of the winter months.

But it was in summer that my tours took place. The ghostly scenes and silence were replaced by the roar of diesel-engined coaches, the changing pitch of camper vans and rental cars as they took full advantage of their gearboxes to climb the short but steep road to the park by the gateway. Accompanying this was the unintelligible blend of a dozen or more languages.

The founders came here first in 1313. How they discovered the site amidst the dense woods, sharp ridges and deep ravines was perhaps the first miracle they sought in their new life. They were a small group of nobles and were led from Siena by one Giovanni Tolomei. They called themselves Olivetans, White Benedictines, and their driving force was to return to the ideals of a simple life that spurred the founding Benedictines. They sought solitude and peace to reflect on their religion and their faith in it. They certainly found the right environment and they began their rebirth as hermits. Tolomei himself, who was to become Bernado or St Benedict, lived in a cave. You pass the small chapel dedicated to him and built near the cave as you come down the steep, cobbled roadway to the monastery with its giant gothic abbey in the shape of a Latin cross. Around this centre-point are smaller churches, chapels dedicated to the saints, cloisters, administrative areas, accommodation for the monks, beautiful arched walkways and balconies, important library and book restoration centres (the monks are renowned for their skills in restoring books and have even established a school to spread those skills) and even a parking and garage complex for a more modern convenience, their motor vehicles.

Modernity has touched the monastery in other ways—a tourist office with brochures on sightseeing in the Siena region, and a small shop selling books, videos and religious objects as well as produce of the monks like honey and olive oil. It is a large operation to maintain and no doubt the Church subsidises it generously.

The external blend of beautiful setting and fine architectural points is matched by the interior—arched walkways, each arch perfectly downsized in proportion as they ascend the three levels of the main abbey building; the magnificent entrance foyer to the library with its vibrant paintings and decorative work on the walls and ceilings and the 'up-and-down' matching curved stairway up to the library door; the massive marble washing trough for hands and dishes at the entrance to the dining room, the 'staff canteen', so to speak; the dining room itself with its pictures and the simple little wooden dining tables lining each wall, dwarfed by the size of the room and the opulence of the whole place.

Most people, however, come to see the five-hundred-year-old frescos covering the walls of the main cloister, *il chiostro grande*. They depict scenes from the life of St Benedict. The first nine are by one artist, Luca Signorelli, and the remaining twenty-seven by the prolific Giovanni Antonio Bazzi, who was nicknamed Sodoma. Examples of his work are scattered in buildings and churches throughout this region. Even the little Romanic church dedicated to St Peter and St Andrew in Trequanda's Piazza Garibaldi has a Sodoma fresco. By all accounts the painter's mischievous character was a perfect counterfoil to his artistic talent. He travelled from commission to commission with an exotic train in his wake: young boys (don't get the wrong impression, he talked of his three wives and thirty children in his letters) and a zoo of 'badgers, apes, dwarf asses, horses . . . magpies, dwarf chickens, tortoises, Indian doves . . .' You can find badgers and magpies in some of his frescos. His style is unique with its lifelike faces, mystically illuminated flowing robes and amateurish backgrounds. After viewing Sodoma's paintings at Monte Oliveto, it's easy to recognise his works anywhere.

Off one corner of the cloister of the abbey is the entrance to the large main church, a high-ceilinged edifice of striking richness. The far apse is a complete little chapel in itself, every square centimetre covered with panelling, paintings, decorations and statuary.

But it is the nave that holds what I think is the real treasure of Monte Oliveto. Lining each wall behind the raised choir stalls are the most stunning series of inlaid wood panels, also dating back five hundred years. The intricacy, shadowing and three-dimensional qualities—the sheer reality of them—is sublimely exquisite. And, remarkable in a church of this stature and size, only a handful of the fifty or so depict religious scenes. Most are scenes of everyday life—a village street fading in perfect perspective into the distance, instruments of the era on shelves in a wall cupboard, a bowl of fruit or flowers on a windowsill . . .

Yet despite this acknowledgement of a secular life outside, and the beauties of Monte Oliveto, I always remained with the thought: the abbey and the Olivetan Order were founded on principles of austerity. Where are they today amidst this paean to the power and wealth of the Church? The inlaid panels alone would probably command a price sufficient to feed the slums of Rio de Janeiro for a year.

It was as we emerged to move on that Aussie Neil made his observation on toilet facilities. Later, I was bemused at how many times a party of, say, four people, needed to use a toilet in a day. Luckily there were pit stops enough where clean toilets were available on the rest of the itinerary.

After Monte Oliveto Maggiore, we drove down into the Val d'Asso and up the hillside of still-nurturing vines that would become Brunello wine, to the castle-dominated village of Montalcino. The castle, at its peak, is a somewhat brutish affair, simple in design—just four high walls around an open space—but elegant enough for its defensive purpose.

Then down the other side is the abbey of Sant'Antimo, older even than Monte Oliveto and a complete contrast with both its open setting in the fields and its bare simplicity inside. I timed the visit to catch the Gregorian chanting by the handful of monks still there. The fifteen-minute service is held six times a day. It seemed odd that the monks needed their prayer books to help them remember the lines; I worked out that at six times a day, they would do the service nearly 2200 times a year. The contrast between the austerity of Sant'Antimo and the opulence of Monte Oliveto was dramatic. My 'people' invariably favoured the austerity; perhaps the rich extravagance of the Church insulted them.

After the steep climb up the foothills of Monte Amiata, and the spectacular views from the ridge road, we descended to Bagno Vignoni for lunch and a footbath in the overflow drain of its town-centre thermal springs.

Then on to Pienza, the 'perfect' Renaissance town of Pope Pius II, who wanted his home village turned into a summer Papal retreat from the Vatican. Leaving, we would stop at the terracotta factory just outside with its huge vases, tabletops and impish statues.

Returning to base, I would stop at the top of the dirt lane to show them where I lived tucked in behind the little wooded rise. To the left, they could see Sinalunga, where most were staying. If we had time, I would take them down to give them an idea of what life was like in a peasant farmhouse during the four hundred years of the share-farming system that died out shortly after World War Two.

Finally, back to Sinalunga, usually between five and 5.30 p.m. They had had a long day but a varied one that covered a lot of southern Tuscany scenery, history, architecture and lifestyles. Every tour party seemed to enjoy it. I was exhausted from the driving, talking, pointing and general shepherding. It required a fair degree of concentration and full-on responsibility for some eight hours.

And it was an interesting reflection on this part of Tuscany that, after those eight hours on its roads driving one hundred and twenty kilometres and passing through fifteen significant towns, villages or major tourist attractions, there was not a single set of traffic lights.

Four

The strip show for all the family

TUSCANY has more festivals than there are saint days on its Catholic calendar. Some, like the Easter procession at Foiano, are occasions for the whole town to display its faith or its solidarity. Others feature keenly contested competitions between the *contrade*, or districts of the town—the Palio of Siena is the Everest of these but there are lesser mountains like the barrel race of Montepulciano, the donkey race of Torrita di Siena and the trolley race of Sinalunga. Each year, the Democratic Left Party—the renamed Party of the Communists who have ruled here for decades—a sort of wolf in lamb's clothing, depending on one's taste in politics—shows its solidarity with the people by putting on a modest festival in every town, village and hamlet around us. Even tiny Rigaiolo, crouched humbly beneath the haughty heights of Sinalunga, merits a *Unità* show for the handful of old Italians who inhabit its few dozen houses. The Party also sets up festival shop next to its headquarters in Sinalunga; our regular

Friday watering hole is underneath Party HQ. The tents and stands are erected on the gravel parking area alongside what serves as car space when the local Sinalunga football team has a home game in the field beyond.

These festivals are very much hit-or-miss affairs.

Some are desperately boring—a quick stroll around the village, a few stalls selling food, a march through by the local brass band, some limp flags for colour and then back home.

Others are blatantly commercial. The annual pecorino (ewe's milk) cheese fair in Pienza is little more than an opportunity for food retailers to set up a stall outside their shop to hook even more wallets from the endless stream of tourists who roam its narrow main street.

But we persevere and gradually discover nuggets of festival gold among the rocks. Among them was the Sinalunga *Festa dell'Unità* strip show.

Everyone enjoyed the show; it was real family entertainment for all including grandma, granddad, the grandkids and the young teens (divided by sex and the catwalk). Even better, it was free.

Solidarity with the masses: in a country where *sesso*, sex, not so much sells as permeates life, what better way to promote your politics than with G-strings and boobs? It is a curious contradiction in the homeland of the Catholic Church. But then, wasn't the Inquisition? So one June Friday evening Nancy and I took ourselves to opening night of the 33rd *Festa dell'Unità*, a ten-day festival hosted by the *Democratici di Sinistra*. Tents and rides and blow-up slides were set up in the parking space between our Friday bar and the Party-sponsored football stadium.

It was not so much curtain rise on the *festa* but clothing drop. It seemed totally unreal, a left-wing political organisation 'exploiting' bodies and the whole family invited. I guess that at least demonstrated class equality. We had read about the show after discovering the advertising poster at La Divina Commedia the previous week. We asked the barman how much it cost. 'Niente, tutti sono brutti,' he told us. 'Nothing, they're all ugly.'

Laura thought the show would be 'tacky and sleazy'. Steve thought his Rosaria wouldn't want to come to 'that sort of thing'.

But we were resolute to see our first communist-sponsored Italian strip show, which was also impressively promoted as 'Internazionale'.

The festival programme had some PR for the sponsors. It said that the organisation wanted to create a heritage for the future, that the Italian Left, *La Sinistra Italiana*, always recognises Solidarity, Social Equality, Democracy, Liberty, Respect, Recognition and Validation of Diversity (the Party's capital letters).

Noble words, noble thoughts. But the hundreds of people who began to teem into the open-air arena that Friday night had more worldly matters on their minds—naked flesh, bare breasts, nipples, bulging G-strings . . . maybe the whole works? And to help get them in the mood, the bar's wine was great. Not necessarily its quality, but the price—1000 lire (about $NZ1.00) for a tall water-glass full, cheaper even than the thimbleful cups of espresso coffee.

The show was just starting as we finished our wine and sauntered past the donation jar into the festival grounds.

A crowd of three or four hundred surrounded the three sides of the catwalk and front of the stage behind. The teenagers had been the clever ones, snaring the front row seats along the two long sides of the walkway—giggly girls on one side, macho boys on the other. I went one better and asked the MC—a paunchy, slimy-looking guy who chain-smoked thin white cigarettes throughout the show—if I could get up on the stage to take photos. *Non problema*. I had a stage-side view of the flesh for the next hour along with the sound man and trouble-shooter who was there to pick up the discarded clothes and make sure no excited hands touched the bodies as they strutted up and down the walkway.

The audience age ranged from babies in pushchairs to pensioners in their seventies or even eighties. They clapped, they cheered, they laughed. It was a scene I simply could not imagine in staid New Zealand, prim England or Bible Belt America; there, it would be a closed door and strict age limit event—and most certainly no grandparents.

The first stripper was billed as an American (remember, this was an 'international' event) dressed in a virgin-white corset affair. Then came a 'French' guy, an Italian girl (Nancy the next day—'Her boobs had to have been bought') and an American stud before the grand finale by a tall 'Brazilian' woman with incredibly tiny boobs (Nancy again: 'The guys had bigger chests').

I even became part of the troupe for a brief moment. As I stood at the rear of the stage, the Italian woman with the store- or hospital-bought boobs shimmied up to me and danced around me a few times. My main impression was of her thick coating of oil, presumably to give her a sheen.

The grand finale even had audience participation. Our Brazilian woman strutted her stuff, tiny as it was, as she shed a gauzy red nightie and red bra then went looking for a man in the audience. It took her a while as the men she approached played very hard to get. From my elevated vantage point I noticed Nancy grab the arm of a man standing next to her, trying to thrust him into the searching stripper's arms. He ran behind the tree line at the back like Michael Schumacher driving a Ferrari.

Finally, a young teen, maybe fourteen or fifteen, was thrust up to the catwalk by his mates. He was quite a well-built kid and had one of those sappy grins that teenagers get when they're nervous or in some embarrassing situation. And climbing up to do goodness knows what with a bare-breasted woman in a G-string in front of your mates and a few hundred other folk—it doesn't get much more embarrassing than that. You had to feel sorry for the hapless kid, even if his mates clearly didn't.

She plonked the kid into a folding chair, straddled his groin area and performed a few bumps and grinds over him. His mates were going wild with hoots and cheers.

She got him to lie flat, face up, on the catwalk and again performed simulated sex as she squatted over him. All this was obviously thirsty work and she needed a drink of water she collected from the back of the stage while the kid lay on the boards getting hand slaps from his mates at the side. The squatting must have taken its toll on her thighs too; this time she simply stood over her supine toy boy—right over his bulging eyes. The view must have been an interesting one, even with a G-string. As she finished taking a drink from the bottle, she spilled some water down onto the poor kid's face to the roar of laughter and approval from the audience. Maybe it was to cool down any ardour that may have been building up? But if so she still hadn't finished with him.

Phase Two in the 'seduction' of a young teenager began with the body lotion. Another stroll—strut, really in best stripper fashion—to the back of the stage. Now to business on the kid, pull up the shirt over his chest, spread some lotion on him, rub it in, stand up, squeeze some on your boobs, rub that in, squat and straddle the kid's groin area—this time facing away from him, a few quick up-and-downs . . . Now let's get the kid even more involved. Grab his wrists, bring them round to your front, get his hands on your chest. Uh, oh! The kid's hands jerked away as if he'd touched acid. Try again, but this time keep a firm grip on his hands and force them to slide up and down over your nipples. More cheers, more applause, more laughs. She knew how to play the crowd.

A final indignity—a 'horrified' peek down his trousers while sitting on his stomach. Then another drink of water and it's time to get up—and tip over the water bottle so it ran down into his pants. No doubt he'd also be having wet dreams as well later that night—and still be boring his own grandchildren fifty years on about his night with a stripper.

Now, as a climax, so to speak, the people got to have their say. This was a communist event, after all, and the voice of the people obviously was a necessary part of it. One by one, the strippers paraded back down the catwalk while the MC tried to rev up a vote by applause count. Of the guys, the 'American' won hands (trousers?) down; maybe it was the thigh-length horse chaps he wore, like those feathery leg decorations you see Zulus wearing on the travel documentaries. No prizes for guessing the female winner—Miss Store-Bought Boobs herself, draped in the Italian flag. That result sent everyone home in a contented enough frame of mind.

It would be completely false to describe the evening's entertainment as sleazy, dirty, disgusting, prurient, offensive, crude or an evil influence on young minds—all those adjectives so commonly used to describe a strip show. It was bizarre, yes, because of its organisers. It was amateurish too. But, hey, this was downtown Sinalunga in rural Tuscany, not the Crazy Horse Saloon in sophisticated Paris. It was, in fact, good, clean, healthy and entertaining fun—'One of the best,' was Nancy's observation.

In the following days, 'la festa della gente', the Festival of the People, had a range of activities organised—discos, ballroom dancing exhibitions, a comedy act, and an inevitable political rally . . . it seemed unlikely they'd get the same enthusiastic turnout.

You simply cannot avoid tits-and-bums in Italy. It seems a massive contradiction in the home of conservative Catholicism. In the big cities like Milan and Rome, sure. But here in the Tuscan farming heartland where life changes so slowly it's like stepping back into a time warp?

I'm leafing through the weekly colour magazine with the local edition of the national daily, Corriere di Siena. It has the coming week's TV programmes (for what that's worth), which is the reason we buy it each Friday when there's not another journalists' strike. Presumably others do, too, including families. It has a bit of travel (great photos), a couple of columnists (one with sex and love advice), some political garbage, music and theatre events in Tuscany, a recipe of the week, etc. There's also always a fashion and a body health section; invariably these are an excuse to get some bare flesh flashing. This week's fashion section, for example, features the autumn musts for men. There's a series of photos with a single male staring pensively into the distance like Rodin's Thinker. Draped all around him in each photo is a naked young woman, breasts aplenty showing. Throughout the magazine there are ten or a dozen such displays, not including the ads.

It's the sheer openness of it that amuses and amazes me. The magazine is obviously going to be seen by young kids flicking through it. But no one gives a damn, apparently. Which is probably a very healthy attitude, much like the attitude to drinking—it's always there so no big deal.

All this bare flesh extends from the pages of the television guide onto the screen itself. Prime-time television news always covers the latest fashion house releases. Half the models seem to be semi-exposed, at least. Programmers don't bother editing sex scenes out of movies—and in a country where young children stay up very late, its an odds-on bet that Mum and Dad don't need to worry about telling them about the birds and bees, they're getting a pretty good idea of who does what to whom in their own living rooms.

One particular programme became a firm favourite—our only one in fact, since Italian TV channels are a triumph of banality. It was a battle-of-the-sexes contest show. It was outrageously sexist. It was everything that would have liberals in other countries sending e-mails to the politicians. It was also great fun.

Each week during its short season it would feature two groups of fifty men or women lined up against each other. The audience was made up of one hundred of the opposite sex. The idea was for the audience to vote on which group was the best after selected panel members performed various feats, displayed talent and answered questions.

It was the make-up of the groups that gave the show its entertainment value. One week it might be 'straight' men against gays. Another was 'pants' versus 'skirts' (this show wasn't about women's fashion). Another two shows featured blacks against whites (men one week, women the next). Then there was the ugly–handsome/beautiful face-off. In between, there were 'normal' contests such as city slickers against country folk, Italian versus *stranieri*, and politicians versus the common people.

One segment had four from each panel perform a fashion show. The first wore formal evening wear. Then came leisure wear, followed by disco outfits. The last of the four was the showstopper—underwear or bedroom attire. And there was some pretty racy stuff on show.

Another segment involved a panellist from each side going back through a 'time tunnel' to another era where they had to identify the era, characters from it and perform some feat associated with that era. One night, two males had to collect as many coins of the era from the bottom of a bathtub filled with soapy water and a skimpily-clad model. As one contestant groped around the model's nether regions, she squirmed so much to avoid the searching hands her top slipped down, revealing a very perky breast. She didn't notice but the cameraman obviously did as his lens remained firmly fixed there until that part of the contest was completed.

There were two celebrity guests each week, one for each panel. They acted as a sort of cheerleader but also got involved in some segments. Each week, they and two panellists would respond to an opinion from a member of the audience. The opinions were invariably sexual in nature. On the black women–white women show, the cheerleader celebrity for the former was the mother of supermodel Naomi Campbell. In the opinion segment, one white guy in the audience gave the thumbs down to black women for sex. 'Baby, you just ain't been with the right woman!' was her instant response.

Yes, the Saturday night fever of *Ciao Darwin* was highly contagious. After the second season we were left wondering what other groups the producers could possibly dream up to rival the likes of blacks-versus-whites and straights-versus-gays and still keep the same heavy reliance on sexual context. Group sex lovers against twosomes-only? Masochists against sado-masochists? Over-eighties versus under-twenties? Fatties versus skinnies (they had already covered big boobs versus small boobs in the first season)? The list, like sex, is limited only by your level of creativity.

So too is using sex to sell. Everybody has seen photos of beautiful young women draped over gleaming new cars at motor shows, even if the connection is tenuous. Harleys and horses definitely have sexual overtones. So, clearly, do products like underwear and swimwear.

But a language school?

One evening in Arezzo, Nancy noticed a new poster promoting the foreign language school where she taught English to Italians. The photo it used to entice new students to learn another language showed a voluptuous young blonde woman from the waist up, her arms folded across her heaving breasts, producing a lot of cleavage. The caption under the cleavage read, 'Vieni e discoperla'. Come and discover it. The connection continues to elude me, though the school's name, Top Level, seemed distinctly apt.

Sex as entertainment for the whole family, sex as solidarity with the voters, sex as a fashion statement, sex as educational development . . . it's time for a cold shower.

Five

Easter in Foiano

EASTER 2000—the Millennium Easter—was a memorable
time. It went not with a bang but hundreds of thundering
explosions for the glory of God and the Ascension of Christ.

Good Friday in Italy is a normal working day; shops are open
and bars do their usual brisk trade. If Italy wasn't going to
celebrate Good Friday, we were damned well going to. Nancy and
I threw a party.

There were several reasons but, perversely, none of them had
the remotest connection with Easter. It was just a convenient
time. First the Germans Reiner and Hannalore were going back
to Hamburg, leaving unfinished the renovations on their newly
purchased but ancient house on the old back wall of Foiano della
Chiana, out on a rise in the middle of the valley. They had been
good friends, first to me and then to both of us. It seemed right to
have some sort of farewell. My birthday the following week may
have been more appropriate but they were meant to leave just

after Easter so we brought the joint function forward. Then *Seasons in Tuscany* was to be launched in New Zealand in the week after my birthday so we made it a triple-headed event. And anyway, who needs an excuse to have a party?

It was, we thought, a reasonable success. I was persuaded to read some extracts from my book, a task I undertook reluctantly as I am a nervous public speaker and gabble through words like a buzzsaw through balsa. Joe the German played one of his compositions on the baby grand; I am not a fan of modern classical music but his piece had elements of the traditional classics mixed with a harmonious modern touch. Then British Brenda, from the Miciano apartments below us and also a composer, played selections of pop music from Nancy's stack of guitar music and many people gathered round to sing.

It was the usual United Nations mix of nationalities that congregate at these affairs in the hills and towns around us—English, Irish, Americans, Italians, Germans and Kiwis. No, I wasn't the sole Kiwi; Ken from nearby Scrofiano and his Italian wife attended the affair. The mix varies, but there is always a broth of accents and languages.

The last guests—three women—left at about 3.15 a.m., so by regular party standards I supposed it was a success. These last three regaled us with stories about how they lost their virginity—one standing up in a Tuscan dirt lane; another, inexplicably, surrounded by fashion store mannequins' plastic arms and legs. A twenty-one-year-old staying the weekend sat and gaped disbelievingly as the stories of lust unfolded.

Easter Sunday was an explosive occasion, just as my first Easter Sunday in Tuscany had been, watching the Explosion of the Cart in front of the Duomo, in Florence. There is still, it seems to a *straniero* like me, a confused blending of pagan rites and religious ritual in Italy, or in Tuscany at least. It is as if the fertility rituals of ancient days have threatened the church; this being unacceptable, the church has adopted them and added its own rituals to confer legitimacy. Florence's thunder and lightning is one example. The thousand-year-old abbey of Sant'Antimo, below La Magia estate where I picked the grapes in my first weeks in Tuscany, had carvings of ancient animal forms and gryphons carved in the stone above its door.

Once again I embraced the smoke and fire of a Catholic Easter, but this time I didn't return to Florence. Instead, the drive was just a short distance to Foiano della Chiana for the annual parade of the Christ figure, a life-sized figure supported aloft on solid Tuscan shoulders.

As they left our Good Friday party, Hannalore and Reiner had invited us for lunch on Easter Sunday. 'But come early, 11 a.m., for the procession,' they advised. 'Is big Jesus Christ procession through zee town and then fireworks.'

We parked in the car park outside the high walls of the *centro storico*, the old town centre, where I remembered their apartment to be from the one time I had visited, just after they had bought it. But that was at night and we had approached it from the central piazza in the main street, the other side from our approach this time. As we walked along the base of the imposing walls, perhaps ten metres straight up, with its row of four-storey apartments rising still higher, Nancy asked how we would find it.

'Look for the black laundry,' I joked. Reiner had always been clad in black since we first met. With his tall, lean body and gaunt face with its large hooked nose, he looked very much like the Grim Reaper nickname a mutual friend had given him.

We found the street, a narrow curving lane dominated by stern-faced apartments on each side. As we walked down it, I said, 'I think we've come too far.' Looking back I couldn't recognise theirs; they all seemed identical. Just ahead, though, there was a man leaning out of a first-floor window.

'*I Tedeschi*, the Germans?' I asked him in the hope that he would be aware of his new neighbours. He pointed at the shutter next to him and then back down our route.

'*Blu.*'

We looked back and sure enough there were deep-blue shutters. It wasn't difficult to see them—every other house possessed the ubiquitous green shutters that are so much a part of the hilltop towns. Not only did Reiner's shutters and door sport a new blue coat but he did too. He greeted us in a very stylish new blue linen suit that he had just bought in Arezzo. But blue! This was unheard of and I immediately dubbed him Picasso.

Later, he told us how a town official had come knocking.

'He say, "You must have permit to paint shutters. And you must only have green or brown."'

Reiner rose quickly to the occasion.

'I say it is only, how you say, first coat, protective coat. Waiting for painter. I not know I need a permit. But how silly is this, you need permit to paint shutters?'

'Probably just another way to get tax,' I offered. Italian officialdom is highly inventive in finding ways to tax its citizens.

Reiner had clearly disrupted the town with his daring decor. The *comune*, town council, was upset and if the gruff attitude of the Italian who directed us with *'blu'* was typical, probably the whole town was in an uproar over his nerve in wandering from the official path.

'Probably if you asked on the other side of town for the Germans they'd just say *"blu"*,' opined Laura.

Reiner did not seem at all perturbed about the storm raging in city hall or along the streets of Foiano. He was leaving for Germany shortly and would worry about his paintwork at a later, distant date. The good folk of Foiano would, until then, have to live with it. Or maybe Reiner hoped the town would rise up and repaint the shutters green while he was away, saving him the effort?

We wandered out into the streets to experience Easter, Foiano-style. In fifty metres we reached a street that, further up, opened into a big piazza. On the right, Reiner pointed out the church where they had witnessed an extraordinary ceremony the previous evening.

The church began to fill at about 11.30 p.m. Just before midnight, the doors were closed and locked. Then, at midnight precisely, there were three loud knocks from the outside of the heavy wooden doors. The doors were unlocked and opened. Men carrying a large statue of Jesus rushed into the church. The men carrying Jesus were covered in cloth so that it appeared that Jesus was flying through the church unassisted.

'They run right around church with statue and then out. Is all over in two minutes. Then people leave. Is very strange.'

It did indeed seem a strange event and its religious significance eluded me as much as the bemused Reiner.

Opposite the church, on the other side of the piazza, stood the town hall from which the green-paint shutter permits poured forth. Two rather grand buildings lined each side of the piazza, looking as important as the town hall with its elegant clock tower; miraculously, the clock actually had the right time, something I had never experienced in Tuscany.

The building on the far side was fronted by a gallery with five or six arches opening out to the open space of the piazza. Four strings of paper fireworks were laid along the floor of the gallery. These strings continued around into the street ahead of us, down to an archway some hundred metres away. There, they turned left and continued down a side street. They were obviously an important part of the ceremony we had come to witness.

The archway opened onto a broad flight of steps. Below, there was another open space with yet another church on one side. There was obviously a religious service going on—and an important one, as people were spilling out of the double doors and onto the terrace in front of it.

This was about midday and townspeople had begun gathering in front of the church. They were all kitted out in their Sunday best—suits and ties for the men, dresses for the women. Over the next thirty minutes a sizeable crowd congregated, perhaps two hundred.

Then the town's brass band came marching up the street leading to the church. These bands are very popular in Tuscany and many towns, including Sinalunga, sport one. The annual flower festival at nearby Lucignano features not one but *four* bands, each with a troupe of baton-twirling, mini-skirted marching girls, leading the elaborate and beautiful floats of flowers. Young children, old men, fathers and sons (these seem to be male-only affairs; most tasks here seem to be strictly delineated by sex) came trumpeting and drumming into the arena and, like all those cellphones, stood waiting patiently. You knew the phones were there in force because of their continual and large range of ringing tunes.

The congregation inside the church began spilling out, boosting the size of the outside crowd considerably. Then came the church priests and acolytes, with banners hung high from tall staffs. The doors were closed behind them.

Everyone was still, waiting in hushed expectancy.

Suddenly, on some unseen signal, a string of fireworks, like those lining the streets, exploded to the left of the church. Thundered might be a better word. They had a percussive power that shocked the air and the ears. Flashes of white light burst through the thick smoke that instantly began to swirl. It was all over in five seconds. And still the crowd waited in the sudden quiet while the smoke drifted up in the gentle breeze.

The doors of the church opened and a life-size statue of Christ emerged, hoisted high on the shoulders of four men. They came down the steps and lined up behind the participants of the coming procession. The Christ statue was surrounded by fresh flowers and candles.

The parade moved out along the street in the direction that the band had come from: banner-carriers first, then the band, then the church dignitaries, their faces expressionless with the solemnity of it all. Finally followed the statue.

The procession weaved through the lower streets of the old town. We didn't follow but retraced our steps to the piazza with the fireworks, where the main event would take place. Occasionally, the sound of the band would drift up as it drew nearer, through the main street and its similar piazza, up to the turning just inside one of the old gated entrances to the town.

There it paused for more fireworks; their sharp crack reached us and even though we could not see them and it was a bright, sunny day, the shadowed reflections of the explosions were clearly visible on the walls of the buildings further down the street.

Then it turned left into the street leading up to the piazza where we and a throng of several hundred waited. Such was the density of the crowd that we could only gauge their progress by the lofted banners and increasing loudness of the twenty-strong band.

It was a gallant little troupe. Crowds swarmed in front of them, behind them and on either side. But the drums kept a-drumming, the trumpets kept a-trumpeting and the cornets kept doing whatever it is that they do.

By the time the parade and followers had all crammed into the piazza it was a considerable confusion of jostling people. It was to get worse.

The procession came to a standstill, the band stopped and the crowd again fell silent. Then, from the street to the left by the archway the explosions began. A group of men emerged into the street leading up to the piazza where I stood on the corner by the trails of paper-twisted explosives, hoping to capture it in my camera. The men began striding up the street clearing people back from the explosions which now turned the corner and came into sight. These were serious fireworks, with ground-jarring detonations and vivid flashes of light. They seemed quite suitable to train élite commando forces to become familiar with the sounds of battle.

One man—he must have been the village idiot—was casually walking between the snakes of fireworks, keeping pace just centimetres in front of the flashing explosions. Further back, where the explosions had passed, the archway had vanished behind clouds of smoke.

Gradually this detonating front line worked its way up the street towards us. The roaring and shock waves began jarring the cobblestones beneath me and hammering at my eardrums. I was less than a metre from them as they passed me and turned into the gallery. The air pressure was so intense that I had to stop photographing to press my fingers into my eardrums, like everyone around me.

A final rush down the gallery and—silence. People, nervously smiling, began removing their hands from their ears. Everyone seemed stunned by the experience—the detonations, the flashes, the cordite smoke. There was even some clapping; either in gratitude for the show or that it was over.

But the show wasn't over.

As the saying goes, just when you thought it was safe to go back in the water . . . A rapid series of three more after-explosions ripped through the piazza. Silence again. Then another salvo.

And that was the end of the show. The procession marched once around the piazza and then off back to the church below, the band once again in full flourish. People began drifting off to their houses for an Easter Sunday feast which would no doubt last all afternoon.

'Man, that was wild,' I said to Nancy. The adrenaline released by the whole spectacle was still swirling through me.

'Look at this,' she said, pointing to her ankle.

Her tights were peppered with holes from the paper that encased the fireworks, sort of soft shrapnel delivered with such force that it shredded her tights. Easter Sunday, Foiano-style, was literally a bang-up show, another enthralling look into the world of festivals and religion in Tuscany.

Earlier, as we walked past a bar, a television set inside was showing a live service by Il Papa, the Father, the Pope, from St Peter's in Rome. I had seen such services before—highly formal, heavily ritualised, excessively ornate and interminably long with little involvement by the inevitably huge crowd of worshippers who attend. My Easter Sunday religion was much more of the people—milling crowds, socialising with family and friends, a boisterous brass band and, as the grand finale, a free-fire war zone display.

Nancy's exploded tights confirmed another aspect of the Tuscan attitude towards life. They turn out in hundreds in these small towns for the festivals and carnivals that each has in abundance. Yet there is little in the way of crowd control or safety considerations. The annual float festival at the end of winter in Foiano is another example—towering floats squeeze down the narrow main street while spectators try to force a passageway between them and the buildings. Meanwhile, automated legs and arms dip and dive all around them, just centimetres away.

The Easter Sunday show was the same, just a token sweep-by to move people back a metre or so from the advancing explosions; once the security sweep passed on, people moved back closer.

In countries like New Zealand or England or America, you just know there would be crowd barriers set well back from the action, an army of self-important, white-coated officials and a large contingent of police for riot control or whatever it is so many police are needed for at such events.

Not so here. These festivals are for the people and the people make damned sure they get close to the action, get involved.

Six

Frogs they would a-racing go

$\mathcal{E}$VEN now, some eighteen months after the *Sagra del Ranocchio Chianino* (the Frog Festival of the Chiana Valley), I still cannot for the life of me understand how the World Wildlife Fund decided to go to war for the frogs which, in Tuscany, were frankly a pain in the arse. At San Clemente we had a watering hole for the cattle on each side of the villa; the frogs in summer would start up about 3 p.m. each day and carry on until about 3 a.m. the next.

As a boy, Elario and his siblings went catching them to supplement the family diet. Even now, writing from my new location, the small native frogs set up a dreadful racket each night. Sure, they're comical to watch. But they're also slimy, noisy creatures that rule with their croaks whatever environment they descend upon.

I don't really have anything against them, you understand. But neither do I particularly carry a torch for them. So the WWF campaign still confounds me. There are, to my mind, far more deserving avenues for their efforts in the woods around San Clemente—the wild boars, the delicate little deer, even the dogs left behind by the hunters out to slaughter the boar and deer.

But, no, this year it was frogs.

When I grew up, about eight or nine, something like that, we had a place like Brolio. Except ours was called Mercer. It sat on the left side of the Waikato River on the way south from Auckland to Hamilton. It was a sorry, son-of-a-bitch of a town, absolutely dead; it was as if a curtain of hush had wrapped itself around the town. Nothing moved, nothing stirred, there was never even the sound of a dog peeing against a streetlight pole, let alone a bark. They even built a little loop road around it so you didn't have to, maybe, vanish within it.

Each time we drove round that loop road my stepfather would jokingly threaten that Mercer would be the place we'd retire to. For a young boy from the bright lights of the city, Mercer was a place of darkness and metaphorical death. Mercer! To live there! Dead City! The Ultimate Threat—retirement in Mercer. There are Mercers all over the world, the places where a fun time out is to walk downtown and watch the butcher's new bacon slicer in action. Brolio is the Italian Mercer. The sort of town you miss if you blink while you're driving through it. But it gets its act together once each year.

This year, however, the WWF gloom patrol was going to wreck even that. Never mind the little people, we're here on a Frog Mission.

'Where's the Mayor?'

'Who's in charge here?'

'Well, get him here.'

'We're from the World Wildlife Fund. We want this race stopped.'

'Because it's stressful on the frogs, that's why.'

'And we're important people on an important mission, so you'd better do as we say.'

'Do? Do? What the hell do we care? You sort it out however you want.'

'That many years? Well, it's about time someone like us came along to stop it.'

'Tradition? Who gives a toss about that?'

'That many months to prepare? People from all over Italy? That much to print posters? Well, that was all a waste of time, wasn't it?'

'Okay, so it stops today. You hear us? Good.'

The Year 2000 *Sagra del Ranocchio Chianino* was only the twenty-third in its history. But the race has origins dating back centuries. The town sits on a small ridge, one of the many that bump the plain of the Valdichiana. Over the years the valley floor has often been under water, a virtual swamp. Canals were built to drain it; today you drive past them on the way to Arezzo. Inevitably, these water channels attracted wildlife: dragonflies, beetles, mosquitoes—and frogs. It became a Brolio tradition to visit the canals, catch a few frogs and have them for dinner—part of the peasant's necessarily frugal way of life.

Then in 1977 a group of ten friends from the village decided to go on a frog hunt and have a big collective dinner with the haul.

But they came back with so many frogs that they had a heap of leftovers. Again, the frugality of the country-dweller came into force; rather then just dump them, they rigged a loudspeaker to a car and drove round the town offering them to everyone. So many people turned out on the streets to get this unexpected bonus that the frog gang decided to do it again the next year. And that's how annual festivals are born.

Today, the whole town is involved in one form or another. There's the frogs to be caught—priority one. Then they have to be prepared. There's the pizza oven, naturally. And the equipment for the cooking. There has to be the big marquee—with bar—for the eating. There are the funfair rides for the kids and the video arcade for the teens. There's the dance floor to be brought in for the grown-ups—and the band to be organised to provide the music. There are waiters and waitresses, chefs, bar staff, ticket booth sellers . . . so it grows.

Now it has become an eight-day *festa* over and between two weekends. They will sell seven thousand meals. They will collect fifty thousand frogs. They will have everyone in the village in the action in some way or another.

And this year, on 6 August, Race Day, they will also have the WWF.

Nowadays the people collect the frogs from the River Po, that famous river that bisects northern Italy. Its headwaters are somewhere to the east of *Torino*, Turin, and from there it cuts a more-or-less straight line across Italy to its outlet just south of Venice. From Brolio, it is a drive of more than two hundred and fifty kilometres. So it is a major commitment in terms of time and cost.

But the frogs must be gathered; the festival awaits.

They hunt in teams. At night with boats on the river. They have lamps and nets.

'The lamp, it makes the eyes bulge, the frogs don't move. So you catch them,' says Cesare, one of the original gang of ten and now *il presidente* of the festival.

'It's like when a man sees a beautiful woman. His eyes bulge,' he jokes from behind his little ticket booth where you come to pre-pay for the meal of your choice and your drinks. The tickets you take into the big marquee to redeem them when you are ready.

Then there are the other teams waiting on the banks of the river. One team of three is assigned to cut off the heads and legs of the frogs. Another team, seven or eight people, skin the legs. A third team's duty is to count the legs and put them in water so they can be returned to Brolio and frozen.

Let the *festa* begin!

There are only seventy or eighty families in Brolio. But as Cesare tells me, 'all are involved. The houses are all empty; that's because they are all here.'

Race day is always the last day of the festival. In the week before it there has been entertainment organised, the kind of old-time dancing that Italians still love. One night there's a theatrical group, another night an illusion and magic show. On the day before there is an amateur cyclist race. And there's the food and drink marquee, the really important part of the whole *festa*—frog leg pizza, deep-fried frog legs, the inevitable French fries, other types of pizza, beer and (what else?) wine. I wanted to try frog's leg pizza; wherever else would such an opportunity crop up? And we wanted to see the frog race.

There are actually two types of races on that last day. The frog race itself is at 6.30 in the evening; presumably the organisers now have the experience to pluck likely-looking racers from the thousands collected at the River Po. This is followed by goose races with the birds hauling specially-built little sulkies and followed by jockeys with hands on the reins tied to the birds.

But today, there was to be bad news.

That morning the WWF had descended on tiny Brolio demanding that the frog race be cancelled or the organisers would be hauled to court.

The racing is too stressful on the frogs, they said.

But the goose racing could go ahead, it was not stressful on the birds!

The logic escaped me. The frogs were unfettered by anything but the geese had to tow little carts and be prodded along by their geese jockeys.

It must have been Save the Frog Year in Italy. Later that week, an item in the *International Herald Tribune* noted that animal rights activists were on the warpath against another frog race planned by another village in the province. There did seem to be some validity to the opposition against the second one. The Brolio event was to be run over a modest, roped-off course of about fifty metres. The second was a Palio-type event with four teams from each of the town's districts competing, according to the newspaper, over a five hundred-metre course! The winning team would be the one to prod or cajole the first frog over the finish line, alive. But that was that village's problem—and one they at least had some notice of.

In Brolio, the problem is more pressing; the organisers stare at a disaster. It's Race Day—and the only advance warning they've had is that morning. In hours, thousands of people will begin arriving to watch the races, eat and drink, then dance the night away. There are thousands of servings being prepared, the band has been booked, the disco DJ too, the trophies are lined up outside the officials' tent, the speaker system has been hired and hooked up, and the bar's fully stocked.

So what to do?

Normally, an Italian in this part of the country likes to cruise comfortably through life. Relaxed, plenty of time for family and friends, more so for festivals, even more so for eating. This is particularly true in our area where, for example, getting a tradesman to make a simple repair can be a task of weeks or months.

But faced with a sudden crisis like, say, a broken sewage line, he will respond quickly. If there's an insurmountable problem, he'll find a way to conquer it. Which is probably why Italian tunnellers are renowned for their engineering skills. Whenever he faces a crisis, he will try to solve it with speed, skill, imagination and flair. If an element of humour can be added into the equation, it will be.

We arrived early and parked in the field before walking to the festival area in the same field but backing on to the edge of the town. It was about 2 p.m. on a hot summer's day. Even by then, the frog dilemma had been solved. How they did it with such speed and style I never did find out. The villagers had promised a frog race and, by all the saints, they were going to have one.

Their solution was simple, elegant and good-humoured. Lined up across the car park end of the course was a row of about six brightly painted, child-sized metal wheelbarrows. They might have been ideal for gardening, weeding or leaf raking in a small Italian backyard. Across the tray of each was a raised strip of metal and sitting proudly on these were plastic toy frogs, equally bright. How they had gathered all these on a Sunday morning (Sunday church services, no open shops) is a mystery. They had turned the event into a sort of running race. We were to learn the rules later. In the meantime I was given an engine-room tour of the food preparation area, behind high awnings next to the ticket booth.

It was a busy, hot scene of organised chaos. Under the awnings there was the baker tossing his pizza bases with flourishes in the air. At the barbecue, two men cooked sausages and the famed local steak, *bistecca Fiorentina*—great slabs of thick T-bone steaks from the Chianina bulls, the world's biggest breed—over charcoals. At the oven, the pizza chef fired his bases, ready for the women to spread them with thick tomato sauce and mozzarella before adding the pieces of frog. Another woman laid out plates of melon and prosciutto, the traditional starter course, on a trestle table. In a back room a team of six women stood like the witches of *Macbeth*, stirring a huge vat of simmering oil and frogs legs, new supplies coming from the mountain of raw legs along a side-wall bench.

Meanwhile, away from the kitchen area, bar stewards were uncorking the wine while waitresses laid long tables . . .

It was easy to see why all the village houses were empty; the whole town really was here.

And so to the 'off'. The newly-devised rules had the entrants of each race pick up the wheelbarrow and run it the length of the course. The frog sat atop the cross-strip and each time it fell off, the competitor had to stop and replace it. It was simple in concept but devilishly tricky in practice across a bumpy field that had been ploughed and reploughed over centuries, and with a low, child's-level vehicle to manage.

I was to become something of a Brolio celebrity for the afternoon. I seemed to be the first journalist/writer ever to have shown an interest in the twenty-three year history of the festival. *And* I was from New Zealand. *And* I was taking photographs! As I snapped away, the Master of Ceremonies at the microphone made numerous references to me. There was even an insistence that I take part in one race. That's how I know how difficult a task it was. I managed to finish about mid-pack; at least I wasn't a disgraced last.

But the highlight of the racing was unquestionably the *Corsa delle Oche Chianine con 'Sulky'*—the geese race. It was a riotous affair. There was only one race, unlike the various heats and age-group frog races. Once the race began it was obvious why.

The owners/jockeys carried their geese to the start line where the sulkies and reins were attached. And then the starter's flag. Some of the geese instantly sat down, others waddled off to the side of the course, others actually made progress for a few metres before sitting down. The jockeys begged, cajoled, screamed, flicked the reins in an effort to get their charges on the move to the finish line. But this was bird-decision time and jockey control was obviously lacking. It was an hilarious affair. As the eventual winner (two or three times a previous winner) trailed his goose across the finish line, some geese still remained planted on the ground at the start.

As a racing event, it would not rate a mention on the Class One calendar. That, of course, wasn't the point. In fact, the races themselves were not the point either, merely a lure.

The point, the *whole* point, of the day was to provide an occasion around which the principal Italian social activity could be built. Thus to the food marquee.

Only about a hundred or so watched the races, but by 9 p.m., the tent was packed with hundreds of diners, with a waiting line snaking outside. It was not a particularly memorable meal, but certainly an occasion to remember. I decided to opt for the deep-fried frogs legs and was delivered a huge plateful of the things, each about the length and thinness of a McDonald's French fry, and equally bland. Picture a wishbone from a turkey. Now come down to a chicken. Now imagine a quail wishbone. The frog legs (actually its back half) were even smaller. The breadcrumbs they were fried in provided more sustenance and substance than the meat.

But the food wasn't the point, either. The point was just to be there, enjoying the show, enjoying the sense of community with these hearty people. Some people from afar are loyal followers—one family drives down from Ravenna, about 160 kilometres to the north, each year. The organisers even offer 'to go' packages; someone once ordered twenty meals to take home to friends or family.

So despite the strictures of the WWF, the event was still a roaring success. This year, the village of Brolio would again recoup its costs and make enough profit to replace old equipment or buy new items to add to the festival. That's become as much a part of the event as the frogs. So has the community support the profits provide, such as new gear for the local football team. And every now and then, the whole village goes on a trip paid for by the proceeds. One year they all went to Pompeii, another to Genoa.

I like to conjure up an image of the WWF that evening. They would be sitting out under an awning in a city restaurant. They would be congratulating themselves for saving the world yet again from barbarians. They would be deriding the small little village of Brolio—'yokels and peasants, no culture'. And they would be eating as they sipped delicately at their wine. Pâté de foie gras. Roast goose with a rich wine gravy. Frogs' legs in a nice little garlic sauce.

These latter-day Caesars may have come, they may have seen. But they definitely didn't conquer the spirit of Brolio.

And so the *festival* parade continued through the Tuscan year . . .

Serre di Rapolano is, at first sight, a typical Tuscan hillside town. It is about ten kilometres from Sinalunga on the road to Siena. Turn left off the main road, up the short hill to the outskirts and then walk up into the *centro storico*, the old town, through one of the gates in the wall that was needed to protect it in less peaceful centuries when invasions and war swirled around it.

It is also the only place in Tuscany where we got lost, this little town of perhaps a few hundred souls, smaller even than Trequanda. But its labyrinth of cobbled alleys and stairways defeated us. It was ridiculous and unseemly. By the time we first arrived at Serre di Rapolano we were experienced *stranieri* who had mastered the medieval mazes of towns in cities like Montalcino, Montepulciano and Siena, even Florence. But this town defeated us as, no doubt, it had confounded invaders of old.

Most of the hilltop towns of Tuscany follow a relatively simple town plan—streets going straight up to one central piazza, intersected by layers of streets that circumnavigate at lower levels. And one main street, halved by the piazza, running across the top. Simple.

But Serre di Rapolano had spirals of streets, and the piazza was not at the top but at the midway point. The main piazza was so small that it seemed just another of the many that the streets flowed into. There was no central focus, apart perhaps from the small castle at the very top of the town. It created a confusing maze that defied the town planning logic we were used to.

One of the most confusing towns, it is also one of the most attractive. As you twist and turn and climb its cobbled pathways a constant stream of beauty reveals itself. Each street corner reveals a bright flowerpot of geraniums or a wall coated with climbing roses. Small flights of cobblestoned steps, indented with the passage of people over the centuries, lead from one street level to another or up to a church at the rear of one of the piazzas, each with its old, raised, rounded well. In many ways, it is like beautiful Pienza. But old Pienza is flat. Serre di Rapolano spills up and down its hillside from the small castle that overlooks it, a refuge in times of earlier wars. It has an evocative air of history, an indefinable atmosphere that breathes a sense of the past into you like no other of the old towns we visit is able to do with the same intensity, the same presence of ghosts from the ages. Also particularly striking are the iron balconies that remind us of French ironwork.

The townsfolk sense this, too, and celebrate it each May with their *Serre maggio feste*. This commemorates the Madonna

Ciambragina, a 'beautiful lass' who lived in Cambrai, France, in the second half of the thirteenth century. She married a rich Sienese merchant called Giovanni dei Rossi, who brought her back to Serre di Rapolano.

The village really gets into action with period costume parades, marching bands, dinners, outdoor entertainment and concerts, demonstrations of ancient artisans at work—all with a boisterousness that belies the quiet atmosphere during the rest of the year. Their enthusiasm is matched by the big crowds who flood into the town at each festival, which is spread over two weekends. This is one of the most popular festivals around (although Italians turn out at any hint of a show or party) and hundreds of cars line the roads below the old town, discharging thousands of people to walk up the steep little hill that leads to the gateway into the old part of town. The weekends are the busiest and it seems impossible that the little piece of Tuscan real estate called Rapolano could absorb so many. The crowds are particularly astounding since the town doesn't advertise other than through last-minute posters that give only festival dates.

You enter through the tall, dark opening in the wall that has stood for six, seven, eight centuries or more—and you go back instantly into those long-ago times when knights took their Christianity and swords into righteous battle against the heathens of Islam when serfs were dragooned to their deaths on behalf of an owner and duke who regarded them as nothing but expendable sword- or spear- or arrow-fodder, when the stench of raw sewage and horse dung in the streets mingled with the smoke of the kitchen fires or blacksmith's forge.

Out into the old town and there's the ubiquitous ticket sellers to collect the 10,000 lire ($NZ10) entrance fee. That's one thing that has definitely changed with the passage of time. The organisers only need to lay their money-collection ambush at the handful of three or four entranceways through the old wall. Even the money-collectors are part of the scene with short-sleeved tunics and the sort of short skirt that you see in historical films. It's mid-afternoon and already a sizeable crowd has built up, milling through the streets rather aimlessly, admiring beflowered nooks and crannies, poking their heads into shops, wondering what's going on and when. Well, for starters, there's the local citizenry: here a young boy in tunic and skirt clutching a vicious looking pikestaff, there a knight resplendent in chain mail and wielding a massive broadsword. On this street corner, a potter shapes his clay on his foot-powered wheel. Over there a beautiful young girl sweeps by in her richly coloured and embroidered velvet gown. In this piazza two costumed men in thigh boots pass the time of day, falcons perched on their gloved and outstretched arms. It seems unlikely they're discussing the merits of sword against spear. Maybe it's the town's appliance shop retailer doing a deal with a client over a new model dishwasher.

In another piazza, we pass a stall with the aroma of sausages being cooked over a charcoal brazier, up some narrow steps and into another little piazza, this one very crowded because here's one of the places where you can buy wine and a *panino con porchetta*, a round bread bun filled with the famed Tuscan delicacy of cold spit-roasted pork stuffed with herbs like rosemary and thyme, salt and garlic.

The robust red *vino* costs L3,000 but that includes the brown ceramic drinking goblet it's poured into. This you get to keep as you sit on a low wall in the piazza or wander the streets until you need a refill which will only cost you L1,000. You also get to take it home, which we did—returning next year with goblets in jacket pockets to save the cost. Many don't make it beyond the night; as the evening nears an end, the sound of shattering goblets drifts through the streets as the effects of their contents loosen inhibitions and finger-grips.

At 4 p.m. the sound of trumpets, drums and other instruments in the distance reaches up into our piazza where we are enjoying our wine. In a few minutes the band—in blue-and-silver tunics—appears from the alley below us. Then some eight couples dressed in medieval finery. Rich gowns of blue and crimson and green grace the women, their hair held up with medieval tiaras and clips; flowing gowns and soft caps clothe their escorts. Finally come the soldiers with their armour, iron helmets with nose guards, swords, spears and pikes. The group passes and pirouettes for a few minutes before marching off to another piazza with our applause wishing them a safe passage.

What gives the festival its magic is the fact that at night the town's electric lights are turned off and the only public lighting is from small oil lamps on the walls of the buildings. It casts an ethereal and warm glow over the streets, a soft yellow haze that allows you to drift back to medieval life. Shadows, glimmers, patterns on the walls of houses, the smell of barbecued sausages, wine from ceramic beakers—all are enriched by the period costumes the townsfolk wear. There is no pollution from artificial lights—you can gaze up and see the stars while you are sipping your wine and eating your *panino* on the low wall in the piazza, waiting for the procession to emerge from the castle and stroll through the maze of cobbled streets. It is a stately procession, the women as graceful as gliding swans and the men proud and strong in their costumes and bearing their fearsome weapons of war. The crowd packs the little streets and alleys, casting eerie shadows on the ancient walls. It eddies and whirls like a stream around rocks. It is alive with talk and laughter, a buzz that we have come to recognise easily in festival-mad Tuscany.

In this atmosphere, it is not hard to cast back all those centuries to imagine a bustling medieval village protected by the lord in his lofty castle. Perhaps the lord and his nobles are eating lustily from haunches of roasted boar or deer, tossing the bones to the baying hounds behind them. A touring team of entertainers may be beside the huge blazing fire, dancing and playing their instruments for the nobles' favour. Below their windows, the hubbub of the town will be drifting up from the maze—hawkers, the strident clang of the blacksmith's hammer, the cackle of the village crones as they swap gossip, the clatter of the horseshoes on the cobbles, smoke and sizzle from the braziers as they cook sausages or rabbits caught in the fields that day, the slosh of a chamber pot's contents flung from a window to the street below . . . the Nights of Serre are evocative ones indeed.

Seven

Intruders

THE farm that surrounds us supports a herd of Chianina cows, the heaviest cattle known to mankind, or so the locals claim. I can believe them. The breed was actually developed in nearby Torrita di Siena where the grateful residents have erected a statue honouring the man who first created them, Frankenstein-like, in the Valdichiana (Valley of the Chiana River, hence Chianina) directly below us.

They are enormous beasts, pure white except, inexplicably, a fawn colour when they are calves. The heaviest bull recorded was a 1750 kg behemoth and that is an awful lot of *bistecca Fiorentina*, the giant 2 kg T-bone steaks that should always be made from the beef of the Chianina.

The farm has a regular herd of some four hundred of these *bestiame* or cattle. Sensibly, like its crops, it rotates them from field to field in the months when the weather is warm enough to release them from their winter lodgings.

They may be big, but they are not particularly bright and follow a rigid pattern each day in a particular field. You can set your clock by their migration routine as they move across the landscape. In the field that runs up to the fenceline of San Clemente's grounds, for example, they will move to the frog pond at, say, 10 a.m. for water. They will then drift up the hill and by 11 or 11.30 a.m. can be found exploring the abandoned ground-level stalls at Casa Nova, from the days when the peasants lived above the animals. At the peak of the summer heat, when temperatures are in the high thirties, they form a pack further back down the hill in the open when there is a small wooded area offering shade perhaps fifty metres further on. They are like robots, big and dumb and following the drum of some herd instinct too strong to allow a sensible course of action. Even in New Zealand, sheep will seek the shade of a tree in summer— and they are not renowned as creative thinkers.

For some weeks in late spring or early summer the farm management put a small herd of thirteen Chianina into the field that lies across the dirt lane from us. Their patterned day started in one corner where they spent the night. They then moved up the hill and down into the gully where a small stream carries winter rain run-off away but dries out completely in summer. By midday they would come back up from the gully to the part of the field that we can look out on from our kitchen and downstairs loo windows to where the frog pond is dug. By nightfall, they are back at their sleeping area. These animals are extremely valuable and each day Santi, the farm manager whose rank allows him the privilege of living in the castle at Trequanda, would drive by to count his herd, to make sure he still had his thirteen charges safely behind the wire cage of the fence.

Finally, after weeks of noting his daily rough ride in the small Fiat Panda over the rutted lane, we offered to do the job for him to save his car and his backside from the jolting. We would ring him if the baker's dozen became a plain dozen overnight.

He seemed grateful for the offer but said that the very next day, he was in fact moving them to a greener field. Certainly they had chewed their way through the field in the preceding weeks and the fodder was looking somewhat forlorn.

That same night, when Nancy had gone to bed to read I stayed downstairs to have a last cigarette. As I stood at the loo having a bedtime pee, gazing into the dark of the night, a white spectre began to emerge into the faint gleam thrown by the outside light we leave on to deter burglars.

This spectre—as white as the marble from the mountains of Carrara on the northern border of Tuscany—moved! It had physical form! It was big! It was a Chianina cow! And it was on our front lawn!

This can't be right, I thought rather stupidly. I moved cautiously outside and poked my head around the corner of the villa. Yep, Chianina cow. It was happily enjoying the grass that was obviously greener on the other side—our side—of the lane.

I called up to Nancy, 'There's a cow on the front lawn.'

A moment later, after she had had a look from an (infinitely safer) upstairs window, she called back, 'No there isn't, there's seven!'

This was a problem, a big one. A problem weighing nearly eight tonnes. As a city-bred character there was no way I was even going to attempt to herd them. What would I do with them if I got them off San Clemente?

I obviously needed help, expert help. And the nearest expert help—and interested party—was five kilometres away in Trequanda. As it was still only 10.45 p.m. I decided that I would just hand over the problem to Santi in the castle. They were, after all, his charges. And farmers, even farm managers, are used to being out at all hours rescuing sheep, shoring up dams, drinking at the local.

The decision made, I took myself to Trequanda. Nancy, the ever sensible and practical scientist, went to bed.

I had no idea what door to knock on to draw Santi from the daunting thickness of the castle walls. It was not a problem I had had cause to encounter in New Zealand or anywhere else for that matter. So I decided the Bar la Siesta would provide the solution, just a few metres across the Piazza Garibaldi from those imposing walls. Surely someone there would know which was the front door, if in fact front doors are a thing that castles have.

Here, the bad-news night took a change for the better. Sitting at an outside table over a drink and a conversation was Santi amidst a group of other locals; I recognised one as a farm employee.

'*Le bestiame è libero*', I told him in my tortured Italian.

Fortunately, he understood me. Less fortunately, he didn't believe me. He plainly thought I was a crazed *straniero*, drunk or just pulling his leg after our offer earlier in the day.

'*No, no. È libero,*' I insisted. '*A San Clemente.*'

Luckily, the farmhand could see the panic in my eyes and urgency in my voice. He said something to Santi, the gist of which took the smile of disbelief off his face.

'*È vero?*' he asked. 'It's true?'

'*È vero,*' I replied, relieved that I was getting his attention.

'*Andiamo,*' he said to his farm worker. 'Let's go.'

This, you will surely understand, was of no little relief. By the time I got back, the cattle had wandered down the lane. But a carful of five farmhands quickly rounded them up back into the field; the cowboys then joined me for a glass of wine before heading off to bed.

It was with some surprise in the last summer of the millennium that we discovered a flock of sheep let loose on the field between our nearest neighbours and ourselves. I think a sheep farmer must have come to some monetary agreement with the farm to lease the land for grazing.

The sheep observed the same predictable routine as the Chianina, moving over the field in a regular daily pattern. But they followed no inner clock. Rather, they were coaxed along by an extraordinary band of shepherds—large white-furred dogs that herded them without any need for human assistance. There were about six of these dogs. They would move the sheep to a fresh patch in the field and then sit, alert but quiet, on the fringes of the flock. At some unbarked but understood time, they would then get up and begin jockeying the sheep along. In this way, the whole field would be covered in a day. The sheep did however manage to slip by their guardians quite often so the owner had to keep a close eye on them.

Each sheep had a bell round its neck and the noise would gradually rise as they moved up the hill towards our fence around midday. One day the canine teamwork went, so to speak, to the dogs.

Nancy awoke to the sound of bells. 'Allan, there's sheep in the yard,' she said as she got out of bed and looked out of our bedroom window.

Yes there were—a hundred or two, happily grazing on our back lawn. They covered it like patches of snow or fluffy clouds that had come to land for a rest. Their dog shepherds were obviously quite content with the whole thing; they had a fence line to keep their charges corralled so they could take watchdog duty a little easier.

The sheep stayed about an hour before our guests and Nancy herded them out through the hole in the fence we had never noticed before—after the dogs had stopped barking at them to steer clear of their charges.

For days afterwards, we walked warily across the lawn, avoiding the pellets they left us as a reminder of their impromptu garden party.

Another visitor also ravaged our plant life; he came unannounced and left just as mysteriously. In the three days with us, he was merciless to Nancy's garden. He ate the tops of leeks, fennel and carrots with a clear-felling precision that the successful contractor is now using to gut the woods of *i monti*, the hills above us.

We called him Doc, but he was more an Ivan, as in the Terrible. I discovered him one day in one of the brick sheds at the back where we keep instruments of torture like the lawn mower and weed eater (weed wacker, in Nancy's foreign language). He was huddled on a scrap of hay or straw that had been there for years. He was sleek, plump and terrified. Doc the rabbit was clearly someone's pet—well-groomed, overfed and too fat to even manage a lope, let alone a gallop like the wild hares we encounter on the roads and in our lane at night.

He was a beautiful creature. His fur gleamed and felt like velvet. It was a coat of black and white that mingled so well that he looked like a lustrous grey pearl in a Fifth Avenue jewellery store.

We fed him carrots and other vegetables in the hope that he would stop plundering the garden at nights. I brought him in and sat him on my knee as we watched Italian television. At least he didn't have the bad house manners to relieve himself on me; this was a house-trained rabbit.

We had only one idea where he could have come from—the centre for troubled kids across the fields. A neighbour worked there so I rang to see if they had a pet rabbit and, if so, whether it was missing.

'No,' she said.

'Well, it's obviously someone's pet but I don't know what to do with it.'

'He'd be good for the pot,' she offered.

Fortunately Doc left before I had to consider such an option. One afternoon he hopped out of his shed, down past the garden he had so thoughtfully pillaged and disappeared around the back corner of the villa and out of our lives.

Whose pet was he? Was he a he? How far had he journeyed? Where was he going? Did he survive?

Such are the questions of the ever-intriguing life we have made in rural Tuscany.

The parade of defecators continued.

I was serenely reading a book in the sun one afternoon when Nancy came out through the locked courtyard gate.

'There's a German Shepherd in the kitchen.'

She had been sitting at our San Clemente control centre, the kitchen table, when she heard a familiar clacking sound on the tiles in the foyer.

'It sounded just like Molly used to when she walked across the tiles,' she said later. Molly, our aged and loyal German Shepherd, had recently died so the memory of her nails on the terracotta tiles was still fresh. Nancy looked up to see a German Shepherd standing in the kitchen doorway, eagerly looking in. Nervously and cautiously, she got up from the chair, backed out of the door leading to the courtyard and came to warn me.

Just as I was getting up to investigate, the Shepherd and his mate, a smaller dog, came bounding around the corner of the house and up to us, tongues flapping in the breeze and tails wagging with enough vigour to create one.

They stayed with us for an afternoon. The little dog was female. She was as bright as a button, her coat the russet colour so beloved by Italian women whose own hair is similarly shaded. The German Shepherd was, to put it mildly, as thick as a brick. He was also very randy and most of his afternoon was spent either trying to mount his companion (unsuccessfully) or in presumed canine frustration, licking his large pink penis that refused to retire into its pouch.

His tongue lolled out of the side of his mouth, making him look as stupid as he was. They were like city kids on a field trip to the countryside. They swam and chased frogs in the pond, tormented lizards and frolicked around as if relieved to be out of the city.

They, like Doc, were well groomed, well fed and came from a good home. Whose, we had no idea.

We had to go out that evening and left them to it on the front lawn, the German Shepherd still pursuing his *amore*, she stoutly defending her reputation.

They had gone when we returned. Again, like Doc, where had they come from? Where were they going? Did they survive? I doubt that the thick male would have lasted a night in the wild without the little female, the object of his lust.

Other visitors came—a cat and a bat—and, after a brief scenic tour of the downstairs rooms, left quickly. At times it felt like we were running some safe house for runaway animals. But none of these compared to the menace I had faced so courageously in my first weeks at San Clemente. The Invasion of the Oven Mitt Snatchers, aka the Great Mouse War.

As the cold weather began fingering its way to *sotto i monti*, the local population of fieldmice decided it was time to pack away their summertime outdoor lifestyle and move to a warmer clime—the kitchen of San Clemente.

The first signs of this invasion force were numerous piles of droppings scattered around the kitchen each morning as I came down to face a new day—on the floor by the fridge, on the shelves with the dried food, on the kitchen bench.

Then they started getting hungry and, for the first time, I understood why previous occupants had unpacked foodstuffs from their paper packaging and stored them in jars or metal containers. The mouse-delicacy type of food anyway—rice, flour, bread, nice cheese crackers. For some reason they showed no interest in the pasta, perhaps because the crinkly, hard cellophane packaging alarmed them when they tried to work through it. At first, I was not too alarmed, being somewhat of a greenhorn in the mousing field.

But that changed quickly when I started to notice scraps of chewed-up paper strewn on the floor. Clearly, the mice were settling in to create a nice comfy home with maybe some cute little baby mice to make it a happy one.

And so the Great Mouse War began.

It was to be a much longer and lonelier campaign than I would have imagined. I came to know how American GIs must have felt during the Vietnam War. There was no frontline; you were fighting an unseen foe and the enemy ruled the night.

I can do no more to describe the frustration, the sense of defeat and the brief moments of sweet victory than to record extracts from my diary during those dark days.

October 13: And is if I didn't have enough flying, creeping, crawling bugs, insects and reptiles to worry about, I now have rats and mice. Not only can I be poisoned, scratched, bitten, stung, but do I also face the risk of some affliction like rabies or the plague?

Well, at least a rat and a mouse. I have surprised them in the kitchen over the last two days and evenings. They seem to have a particular liking for flour and biscuits. So today I have been to the Emporium in Trequanda to get some rat poison. The young man showed me two choices and recommended one as 'Is best'. And today I will turn hunter, scattering some of the sachets in the places I have surprised my predators—on the shelves, on the kitchen bench and behind the deep freezer and washing machine.

October 14: Well, my skills as a hunter leave much to be desired. With eager anticipation I entered the kitchen expecting to find, if not dead rodent carcasses, then at least some of my carefully planted rat poison sachets either gone or partially eaten.

Not one had been touched! But on the hopeful side, there were equally no signs that my rat or mouse had invited themselves to dinner.

Perhaps the poison 'is best' because it scares the creatures away; that they are look-and-run sachets rather than eat-and-die. Or maybe they are designed to make the pests laugh themselves to death when they see my feeble efforts to destroy them.

Dispirited, I have decided to put them away tonight and see if there are signs tomorrow of the rodents' return. Expect more reports from the trenches.

October 15: Dispatch from the rat battle front: still no sign of the rodents' return, even though no poison was set.

October 16: The vermin has counterattacked! He/she left the rodent equivalent of land mines once more last night in the kitchen.

And the rat is still having sport with me. As if to show its complete contempt for my feeble showing so far, it left just one sign of its presence; the mouse, at least, had the good grace to leave six or seven traces to remind me of its visit. Tonight I shall set ambush sachets out in no-man's land. We shall beat them on the shelves. We shall beat them on the benches. And we shall beat them behind the whiteware!

October 17: My ambush strategy has been a complete failure. No sign of rodents, no sign of sachet devouring.

I have one last strategy in this campaign—the siege. If it worked for the Trojans, the Medicis, I can only hope it will work here. Simply, I will starve them into submission. I will ensure every morsel, delicacy, taste sensation that they could fantasise about will be withdrawn. Let's see how they like that!

October 29: Grim news, I am afraid to report. I am in desperate retreat. I now know how Napoleon and Hitler felt as their armies fled from the gates of Moscow. On my descent to the kitchen this morning I found that the rodent had certainly eaten my bait, a piece of fine New Zealand cheddar, and set the trap off. The only trouble was, the trap was neatly packed away in an open container on the bottom shelf of my shelving system, while I had perched it overnight on the second-to-top shelf, a metre above. The cheese was gone all right. The trap had been triggered. But no rodent! It was as if the mouse had liked my dinner offering so much that it wanted to thank me by washing the dishes and putting them away. How humiliating!

November 1: I am still in headlong flight. On Wednesday night I reset the mousetrap with more cheese. In the morning, the cheese was gone but the trap was still set. I forgot to put more cheese out on Thursday night, but on Friday morning, the trap had been sprung, despite the absence of dinner for the mouse. What does this mean? And another alarming trend has emerged; on both mornings, a packet of coffee filter papers was lying on the floor beneath the shelves! Is the mouse now so arrogant that it is demanding after-dinner coffee?

November 8: One triumph. I have supped at the cup of sweet victory and it tastes just fine.

Last night, I reset the mousetrap after an absence of a few nights and, lo, there was the mouse well and truly kaput this morning. Perhaps he/she just got too cocky and overconfident.

And so, the battle of the rodent closes—27 days after we first locked eyes. That is, of course, unless there are more in my kitchen!

November 17: Disastrous news from the rodent front: at least one is back and it is being very aggressive. It has stolen my oven mitts, tried to steal my hand towels and tea towels and takes cheese from the set trap without concern. This is a lonely and tiring battle I wage.

November 20: My rodent still lurks in the kitchen. I managed to grab his tail hanging down below a shelf one day but could not get a good purchase and he scooted behind the fridge. He even invaded our dining room while we ate one evening (this on Nancy's second visit). At night I hear sounds of his presence below—a clanging or crashing—and in the morning find items like spice jars either knocked over or on the floor. He must be getting hungry for I think I have locked or closed all food away.

This beast is making a mockery of me but I intend to emerge victorious.

November 26: I have had some successes on the rodent front. I reverted back to the poison but this time closed both kitchen doors and dusted the poison with flour. Both last night and the night before, the bait has been taken. So I am hopeful that this will be resolved shortly. I will, however, continue laying the poison.

December 2: I now have four mice to my credit—one by the trap, one I trapped in the bathroom last Friday night and two by poison (one of which still managed to bite me so I am waiting to see if I develop a rabid fear of water). There has been no sign of them in the kitchen now for some days, but the fruit bowl in the dining room is under attack and Carlo noticed signs of them in the upstairs library. So I am now renewing the battle on two fronts, buoyed by my success in the kitchen.

Over coming months, though, I was to find occasional reminders to bring back the memories. One day in early January, I was cleaning the gas jets under the kitchen hob. My hand rested upon a pile of shredded vinyl contact paper (the sort you use to line kitchen shelves and cupboards) in a corner under the hob. Fearing the fire risk I began pulling it out to dispose of it. And along with the paper came a cindered mouse tail! That was all. No sign of the rest of the mouse, which I can only assume was vaporised by the heat of the gas burners. Later that month, I decided to freshen up all the bed linen stored in a big chest in one of the bedrooms upstairs. As I cleared the linen from the top drawer, I saw the base was littered with little splinters of wood. Then as I opened out one sheet I discovered the desiccated husk of another mouse, which had obviously been dead for many, many months, if not years. How it got into a closed drawer I can only surmise—somehow squeezing through a crack. Or climbing up a gap between the back of the dresser and the drawer ends. Or perhaps grabbing an instant opportunity to establish a cosy nest while the drawer was left opened one day. The splinters of wood and teeth marks on the inside of the drawer were, I can only assume again, signs of frenzied efforts to escape from its nest-turned-prison before giving up and retreating to a folded sheet to die.

If my Mouse War was over, another was about to begin.

In January, my neighbours Airdrie, Angela and Sam, whose house I can see up the road from San Clemente, were also invaded by mice. Not bothering with the type of frustrating tactics I adopted, they called in the heavy artillery—the local rat-catcher.

He duly laid traps with poison bait around various upstairs rooms. He took a particular interest in Sam's bedroom where there were apparently signs of considerable rodent activity. With military-like precision, he placed one bait trap behind her bedhead.

And so for the next couple of weeks, she had to endure the sound of scuffling mice beneath her head each night. One night she rolled over and found a dead mouse on the pillow beside her. Another, she woke to find a groggy mouse weaving across the floor, also headed for her bed.

These—and my own experience—seemed to belie the assurances of the rat-catcher and others that the poison makes the mice thirsty and they will go off to find water and then die elsewhere. Certainly the three I killed with poison all turned up in their final death throes in my kitchen.

One mouse obviously died in Sam's room. The smell, she said, was ghastly but try as they might, they could not find the body and she had to endure the odour of decaying mouse flesh each night for some time. But like good generals, we determined to learn from our experiences and be better prepared and better armed the next autumn.

My own private little war continued for another few days. But now I was assured of winning. I was to find one more poison-groggy mouse in the kitchen but none upstairs.

Total victory was mine. It was a heady feeling.

Terza Parte

Places to go

Chi vuol far roba, esca di casa.
Who wants to create things,
must leave the house.

—*Tuscan proverb*

Eight

Byron's Grotto and the Five Lands

BYRON used to sit there on the wall, watching the waves continue their aeons-old assault that carved the grotto at the base of the steep cliff. Perhaps composing his poetry. It is certainly a view that inspires.

Later, further down the Tuscan coast, he was to witness a more macabre scene—the beach bonfire of his friend and poet colleague Shelley, drowned while sailing up the coast to see Byron at this little village of Portovenere.

His body washed up two weeks later. Shelley's friends decided to cremate him there. A witness described the scene as the group stood around the bonfire of the poet 'pouring libations of wine, salt, and frankincense on to the red-hot ashes'.

'. . . the brain literally seethed, bubbled and boiled as in a cauldron . . .' The gruesome story has it that somehow the poet's heart remained unscorched and intact, so it was promptly despatched to England and buried at Bournemouth on the south coast.

Today, you can sit at the stone wall along the side of the walk up to the headland. It's too high to look over, I imagine for safety reasons, as it's a straight drop down seven metres to the rocks below. But there's a little window-like opening built into the wall. Through it, you can see the cave across the cove. They call it Byron's Grotto and there's a plaque commemorating his visits to sit at the wall. Below me, in the water, swimmers use the surge of the sea swells to fling them back up on to the big rocks. Even on a calm, sunny day in early September, those swells demonstrate the power of the Mediterranean; the winter storms must be ferocious. Byron sat here nearly two hundred years ago; it may be a romantic notion, but I have no doubts that he too looked down on swimmers leaping with the sea's surge like salmon up a waterfall.

Perhaps it was here that he composed his homage to Botticelli's *Birth of Venus*, perhaps the most famous of the artworks in the Uffizi of Florence.

We gaze and turn away and know not where,
Dazzled and drunk with beauty, till the heart
Reels with its fullness . . . chain'd to the chariot of
    triumphal Art,
We stand as captives and would not depart.

The marketing people have done their job well. They promote this part of the Italian coast as 'The Gulf of the Poets'. And not without some justification. Byron, Shelley, Dylan Thomas, Milton, Dante . . . the great verse-makers were all here.

As Byron observed:

What men call gallantry and gods adultery,
is much more common where the climate's sultry.

So too did the writers come: Dickens, Smollett, Aldous Huxley, Trollope, Dostoevsky (his dark side would have relished the brooding streets of Florence), Mark Twain, D.H. Lawrence and, in more recent times, Ernest Hemingway.

Shelley called it a Paradise of Exiles; a parade might be a better word.

Portovenere is not actually in Tuscany, but it's within the throwing distance of a Chianti bottle, just over the northern border where Tuscany becomes Liguria, the Italian Riviera. We wanted to see the little fishing villages renowned as Cinque Terre, the Five Lands, on this part of the steeply-cliffed coast. Portovenere is not one of the Cinque Terre, but it is the first port village on that coast. It lacks the cachet that the rich and famous give to Portofino still further north. But it is a glorious example of the pastel Riviera. In rural Tuscany the colours of the architecture reflect the peasant's countryside heritage—the grim greys or dusty browns of the stone walls, the coppery terracotta of the tiles, the pure forest greens or oak browns of the shutters' paint. On the coast, that sombre note of a hard rural life changes to a dancing palette of lightness that reflects the changing patterns of the sun on the Mediterranean. Corals, salmons, gentle mustard yellows, soft sea-greens, aquamarines, sky-hazed blues . . . they are an uplifting sight for the spirit. And there is always the blue of the sea they seem to embrace, so close is their marriage to it physically.

Portovenere is about a twenty-minute drive from the major Italian naval base of La Spezia. The latter is a largish city built into the back side of the Gulf of the Poets. At night, groups of uniformed sailors on shore leave roam its streets, looking for companionship. There is also a container port, but in mufti, the sailors from those ships are harder to discern. Apart from the naval base, it has little else of note to recommend it.

'If I was a young Italian woman, I'd get all my girlfriends together and head for here,' enthused Nancy as we walked the streets from our restaurant on our second night.

'You can have your pick. Just point and say, "I'll take you. Or you."'

'And even better, they've all got jobs.'

We actually stayed in La Spezia for our two-night visit. It was an easy drive to Portovenere over the ridged road and there was an efficient train service through the hills to the villages of Cinque Terre—one of those you can hop on and hop off at each town's station, just minutes apart through the tunnels. We had been forewarned about the excessive cost of hotels and restaurants in those little towns as tourists have increasingly discovered the area. So our thin wallets were delighted to accept the free parking (when we finally found it), the cheaper food and wine, the L10,000 one-day train ticket that would allow us to be delivered and picked up anywhere along the Cinque Terre line—like the tunnels along the Autostrada in the Italian Riviera, another testimony to Italian skill—and the L60,000 a night (for the two of us) at the modest one-star Hotel Flavia. It was about halfway up the main drag, the Via del Priore, between the harbour and the railway station, down a narrow little alley off to the left, empty except for broken beer bottles and dogshit. The old woman who ran it lived a pitiful existence. Our room was about three times as large as the cramped little cubicle she occupied next to us on the ground floor. There she sat all day, on her bed (there was no room for a chair), watching television and waiting for customers to knock on the door. From memory, it was about four metres long at most by three wide. It was a sad sentence of solitary confinement to glean a tourist dollar.

Portovenere is on the end of the northern arm of the gulf, up and down and round the hills and curves, past the high barbed-wire-topped walls of the naval base and then a final descent to the sea and the town. Like most Italian towns, and particularly the hill towns of Tuscany, it is in two parts—the old and the new. As you reach the bottom of the hill at the entrance to Portovenere, there's a piazza with a round garden in the middle. Turn left and follow the road and you will come to the new part with its chic restaurants, proper beach, public gardens and high-rise apartment blocks.

But it's the old part, in front of you, that is the lure.

It is basically a town built in tiers. First, the little breakwater harbour where the private fishing boats of the locals vie for mooring space with the yachts and launches of the tourists and the wealthy. Then the marvellous waterfront with its rock sea-wall where sunbathers lie (uncomfortably, it must be said), its wide promenade and a row of six or seven-storied dwellings—pastel-coloured and jammed tightly together like a house of cards, each two rooms wide per storey. They look like they could collapse at any instant, just like the card houses I built as a child. The town has an elegance and beauty together with a graceful indifference to urban planning. The houses are also an historical reminder of the superb strategic position of Portovenere through the centuries. Originally built as watchtowers at the opening of the gulf, today, drying laundry hangs from clotheslines outside the windows rather than flags or alarm torches, restaurants line the ground floor entrances rather than the weapons of war that stood at the ready in the twelfth century when the Republic of Genoa recognised the town's strategic potential. But even as far back as Imperial Rome it was a haven, a safe stopping place for galleys on their way to ancient Gaul or Spain.

Behind this wonderful kaleidoscope of pastels, water, restaurant umbrellas and architectural jumble is another level. The next tier on the steep hill the town rides up is a miracle of mayhem, like all the towns with their typically narrow warren-ways of medieval Italy. Finally you reach the castle at the very top, the strategic heart of old Portovenere. The 'main' street, the first behind the waterfront and about twenty metres above it, is known officially as the Via G. Capellini, but as the 'Carrugio' to the locals. It is only about four hundred metres long but it contains nearly a thousand years of history with its archways, dark alleys and inscribed tiles at the doorways of the shops and houses. We stopped at one grocery store that was an exuberance of colour and asked the shopkeeper inside if we could take a photo. She immediately went behind the big, glassed meat counter and switched on the lights to give us more light for the shot; then she turned all the prosciuttos and cheeses on a 45-degree angle towards the entranceway.

At the end of the 'Carrugio', you emerge from the dark

shadows into the sunlit broad expanse of the Piazza L. Spallanzani. On the left is the entrance to the gulf with the island of Palmaria across the narrow few hundred metres of this northern entrance. On the right is the wall with a window that looks across to Byron's Grotto at the base of the high cliff. Then there is a short climb up a wide rock stairway to the stark little church of San Pietro, right at the very tip of the peninsula. For more than eight centuries it has stood there, a religious lighthouse for sailors seeking safety in a storm. Its origins go back even further, to the sixth century AD. It is a grim place, without the money that the Church has poured into the great cathedrals of Rome or Florence, although it does have the striped black and white marbling style of the Tuscan cathedrals. But its proud position at the edge of the inlet gives it its beauty, wonderfully gilded doors with relief images thrusting out of the metalwork. On three sides, the waves surge and swirl around the rocks some twenty metres below. From its balcony, you can look back to the marble mountains of Carrara or up the jagged coastline where the villages of Cinque Terre were waiting for us. Or you can just gaze out to the sea and wonder where in the summer of 1897 Marconi conducted the experiments that were to herald today's communication age.

As we looked out to sea we noticed a fishing boat coming back to port from the cliffs to the north. It was early evening and the sun was just setting as the little boat ploughed back through the swells.

As a child, I had a storybook about Toot the Tugboat who lived in some upriver port in America. He either escaped or got carried away from Mum and Dad Tugboat and had a series of perilous adventures as he was swept down to the big city at the river's meeting with the sea. The fishing boat below our lookout on the church reminded me of Toot, but without the tugboat's little funnel, just a narrow little cabin for protection.

'Come on, let's go and talk to him,' I said to Nancy.

Maurizio could have been the model for David that Michelangelo sculpted from the block of marble hewn out of the mountain a few kilometres away. By the time we reached the small harbour he was already docked and unloading his gear. No fish; he had just set his nets as he did each evening. He went out to gather them each morning at four-thirty.

He was strikingly handsome, with the superb physique that comes from hard work, but not yet the ravaged face that comes after a lifetime of facing the many furies of the sea.

Our resurrected Neptune was thirty-seven, but looked much younger. Remarkably, he had been fishing these waters for fifteen years. He bought his little Toot ten years ago. Five years ago, there were seven or eight fishermen catching the bream, lobsters, tuna ('*piccolo*', small) and other fish that make a home below the coastline cliffs. Now he is the only one left. He had five nets he set each evening. One was four hundred metres long, the rest three hundred metres. The fishing was best in winter (those storms!) but the prices were highest in summer when the restaurants paid top lire for his fresh catch for their wealthy patrons. But in winter, when the tourists fled back to the central heating, the townsfolk came down to the quay each morning to inspect and buy from his plastic baskets. It was obviously a hard life, but at least it was a year-round one that paid. And that was about the extent of our talk; he was hungry and eager to get home for his meal. Who could blame him?

That night, back in La Spezia, I had a taste of the fresh seafood that Maurizio might have caught—a mixed grill of prawns, a half-lobster, calamari and a fillet of some indeterminate fish. At least it was a luxury of freshly caught and cleaned fish. The Tuscans have a passion for demonstrating the freshness of their produce. The *pomodori*, tomatoes, are sold in clusters of four or five still attached to the stalk. The cultivated *funghi*, mushrooms, still have clumps of the growing mix clinging to the stem. Unfortunately, they do the same with the fish, which are ungutted when you buy them. Obviously no matter how fresh the catch, it takes time to get it delivered from the coast to our inland area. We sometimes bought a fish but invariably the flesh was tainted. Seafood was also expensive. For some reason the little farmed trout were relatively cheap but they were also uncleaned.

The trattoria/pizzeria was emblazoned on the outside with a garish but apt cherry-red lobster in neon. Nancy made the mistake of ordering a pizza. As usual, wherever we were to go in Italy, it was dreadful. We have not been to Naples, the so-called birthplace of the pizza (although I still maintain it is a New York creation), where the pizza is said to be great. But everywhere else we went, the Italian restaurateurs ably demonstrated their complete inability to make a decent pizza. The only redeeming quality, to my palate, was the thin, crusty base.

Cinque Terre, the Five Lands, are five little towns, each with its own flavour, impossibly beautiful with the sea, the sun, the scenery and the setting. Behind them rear high hills terraced for growing grapes and crops—two thousand kilometres of stone walls were built to create the terraces. The drift of the young to the easier life of the city, as in rural Tuscany, has seen the agricultural base all but disappear. But there is still the fishing—and the new economic wave that matches those coming in from the sea, marching down the winding streets from the rail line.

Cinque Terre is both a world heritage site and on the world monuments list of 100 most endangered sites. The biggest danger seems to be that tidal wave of tourists that flows down and through the towns each day—the train that brings them here has to be as long as one of the big Eurostar trains that whizz between Rome and the cities to the north, Paris, London, even Moscow. We were to be part of the swirling waves for a day.

Monterosso al Mare is the northernmost of the Cinque Terre villages and we went there first, planning to backtrack down the coast to the others. It's the most 'open' of the five—a long stretch of wide beach in the new town section before a short climb over a hill topped by the medieval Torre Aurora (Dawn Tower) and down into the old town with its small breakwater harbour. The train from La Spezia takes just over twenty minutes, snaking along the side of the cliff faces falling away to the sea and through the many tunnels that were needed to get through the ridges forming parts of the cliffs.

At the far northern end of the long beach, yet another ridge abruptly cuts off sea-level access to points further north. Into it has been carved a remarkable figure known as *Il Gigante*, the Giant. He is crouched under some heavy weight on his back, perhaps the weight of the rock he has been carved from. His pose looks like those depictions of Atlas straining to stop the Earth plummeting into some hellish abyss, but with his bearded, leathery face seems more like Neptune. He is about twice life-size and why on earth he was hewn from the cliff I have no idea. The beach leading back towards the old town is lined with restaurants and bars. On the sand in front of them, lurid conga lines of beach umbrellas protect the holidaymakers from the sun as they lie on deck chairs. You have to pay for the privilege of using them.

Up and through the short tunnel beneath the Dawn Tower you descend into the old town. The little harbour is a sanctuary for fishing boats and a dropping-off point for the tourist ferries that ply the coast. Old men cast unweighted lines into the water in the way a fly fisherman tries to lure a trout, while a father teaches his young son how to emulate their casting. Back behind the waterfront square with its open-air bars and restaurants and market trucks selling the most ghastly rugs and brassware, the narrow streets wind up to peter out wearily in the battle to conquer the steep cliffs.

The architecture of all these villages is similar—tall, narrow buildings lumped side by side with shops at the street level. We stopped at a bar about halfway up the town. It had two entrances on to the streets that ran down either side of it. Unlike most Italian bars, this one had a theme. Film and music posters adorned its walls—*Apocalypse Now*, Umbria Jazz '95–'96, Jivin' Joe Jackson, The Cure. We figured it must been one of the happening places because of the sign on the walls asking patrons not to sing, whistle, shout, fight or otherwise disturb the night at closing time. The neighbours had obviously been on their case.

Then on to Vernazza, a small outpost jutting out on a rock shelf right into the sea. Another little man-made harbour lies at its base. All streets and alleyways lead down to the sea, opening on to a large piazza on the waterfront. As you walk down those streets from the station you pass fishing boats dragged up from the water and parked in front of shops and homes. Emerging into the square, on the right is the large, towered parish church dedicated to St Margherita di Antiocha. Its beginnings go back to the eleventh century and its foundations are part of the sea wall.

We sat in the piazza under the umbrellas of the bar; behind us in the protected small harbour people swam or dived from the breakwater wall. Later we strolled 'uptown' and had *focaccia* sandwiches at one of the three or four small tables outside a hole-in-the-wall restaurant. The bread was crisp and lightly baked. The word derives from the Latin *focacia* which in turn came from the word *focus*, meaning hearth. The implication of bread being the centre of the house, of life, is unmistakable. It is a mix of flour, water and brewer's yeast. The dough is allowed to rise before being spread on a baking tray greased with olive oil. It is smoothed out so that it is never thicker than two centimetres. It is then flattened a little and spread with salt and olive oil before baking for twenty minutes or so. My choice was a topping of anchovies; Nancy went for the *tonno con pomodori*, tuna with fresh tomatoes. My anchovies, sadly, were so heavily salted that I couldn't finish it; if I had I would probably have had to drink two kegs of beer before night's end.

Then all aboard again and on to Corniglia, the least interesting but certainly most arduous of the Five Lands. The other four villages have the rail line arriving just above the town with only a short walk down into them. Corniglia does spill down to the sea, but on the other side of its clifftop centre from the station. And the centre is high, high up. You have two choices from the station, just a few metres above the shore—walk up the steep, winding road, past the olive groves and grape vines, or up the even steeper stairway of three hundred and sixty-five steps, one for each day of the year. We chose the former to go up, the latter to come down. It was a stiff walk under that midday

Above: Spring poppies advance on a house at the edge of Trequanda.

Below: The old and new. The modernistic statues of Colombian artist Fernando Botero stand watch outside Florence's famous Uffizi Gallery. This amalgam of new art against old is a common, almost impish, delight in Tuscany.

Above left: A lazy afternoon on the launch ramp of Cinque Terre's Manarola. *Above right:* A conga line of umbellas on the beach at Cinque Terre's Monterosso al Mare.

Below: Italy or Ibiza? Nancy paddles at Lago di Bracciano just north of Rome in our last month in Italy.

Above: Renaldo, the essence of rural Tuscany, carves his prosciutto at the kitchen table. Lassi, our Finnish friend (second left), enjoys a glass of the host's wine.

Below: Salamis, prosciutto, sausages and cheeses tempt the palate in Florence's indoor food-market.

Above left: Renaissance man . . . a proud Civetta *contradiolo* readied for the historic parade before the Palio. *Above right:* The Palio crush in Il Campo.

Below: The tables wait for the traditional eve-of-Palio Civetta dinner.

Right: The Dorica castle overlooks the arched, medieval bridge across the Nervia River at Dolceacqua, just inland from the Italian Riviera. The bridge was made famous in scenes by the French Impressionist painter, Claude Monet.

Below left: Byron's Grotto at Portovenere. *Below right:* The modern David . . . Portovenere's sole fisherman back in port after setting his nets for the night.

Above: A Tuscan farmhouse scene.

Below left: Rejuvenated. Cellini's restored masterpiece *Perseus* once again looks over the Piazza del Signoria in Florence. *Below right:* Democracy for all. And sex.

Above left: Maidens grace a float of garlands at Lucignano's Flower Festival.
Above right: The old crone (papier-mâché) who is a traditional part of the colourful parade at Lucignano's Flower Festival.

Below: The flower girl and boy in their float at the Flower Festival.

Above left: Nancy (white jeans/shoes) gets her antipasto at Trequanda's annual outdoor feast in the piazza. *Above right:* Cards and gossip in Sinalunga's Piazza Garibaldi.

Below: Chef Walter selects a wine for a table at l'Amorosa.

(actually, about two o'clock by this time) sun. And the effort was not really worth it. Even the Church (1334) of San Pietro was locked, most unlike Italian churches. The views along the coast from its high elevation were certainly splendid, but the town itself was a bit of a dead place. We were pleased to descend the stairway to head for the fourth of the Cinque Terre.

Manarola was undoubtedly my favourite of the five. It is unbelievably picturesque, this pokey little town that seems to quail on its clifftop above the surging waves below. It cannot even boast a harbour, or a waterfront piazza. The fishermen have to haul the boats up on to a small 'parking area' over the curved, sharp causeway that runs directly down into the sea. The rock causeway has spaced planks of wood to preserve the hulls of their craft. Sunbathers set out their towels on it while others read newspapers sitting on the low stone wall on each side. Above them, the pastel homes climb up and up and up. Even in a gentle Mediterranean summer, the sea surged against the rock cliffs, frustrated by its attempts to wash away man's invasion.

Today, the bright colours of modern sea machines—kayaks, small yachts, inflatables—compete with the fishing caïques for the limited parking space.

For those so inclined there is a pathway along the cliffs between each of the five villages. We took the last section, the Via dell'Amore, Lovers' Walk, from Manarola to the last village, Riomaggiore. It was only a short walk cut out of the hillside and taking perhaps ten minutes, about fifteen metres above the rocky coast. In the late afternoon sun, fishermen were already casting their lines from the rocks below. The cliff walk was quiet with relatively few people, most of those appearing to be locals out for their late afternoon stroll. It was a welcome relief from the tourists. The path leads first to the new town area, then you have to pass through a tunnel network to reach the old town. It has no sheltered harbour, either, just a short, straight launching ramp leading from the end of the main street down into the sea. The town is set into a cleft between two ridges. We climbed to a bar on the top of the southern ridge to watch the sunset. Nancy recalls it as being named the Sunset Bar. It was a beautiful position to see the red sun set below the sea's horizon. Then, promptly after we arrived, the bar announced its close-down for the night. It was ludicrous. Here it was, a beautiful view to the emerging lights of the town, the sound of the sea soughing at the rocks below, a prime spot in town, a warm summer's evening, the height of the tourist season . . . but, no, we were to be denied the pleasure, and they would miss out on the tourist dollars or lire or marks or francs. The logic was unfathomable.

But we had had the sunset at least. So back to La Spezia and the sailor-and-smoke-clogged air of a cellar in La Tavernetta restaurant before departing for San Clemente the next day.

Nine

The other Riviera

$\mathcal{T}$HINK Riviera. Think sun, sand, sea and sensuous skin. Think again.

Think rugged and stark mountains, dark and wooded ravines, plunging cliffs, razorback ridges with tiny villages perched precariously along their thin, sharp spines. Think the other Riviera, the inland one deep in the river valleys and high atop the peaks of the Maritime Alps.

The flat coastal plains and seaward-jutting promontories that border Italy's Mediterranean shore from San Remo to the French border some thirty kilometres away—the 'western gateway to Italy'—are, at most, several kilometres deep. Like its French counterpart so close to the west, this part of the Italian province of Liguria, the furthest part of the Italian Riviera that stretches for hundreds of kilometres from the border to Genoa and down along the thigh of 'the boot' of the Italian peninsula, is mainly popular for its marine attributes—beaches, boating, diving, dramatic cliff scenery, beautiful coastal panoramas, colourful old towns and fishing ports, seaside fish restaurants and promenades . . . But just a few kilometres inland, into the valleys that lead to the steep heights of the *Alpi Marittime*, is another world.

It is not a world of new-age glamour, sex and hedonism. Rather, it is an old world of ancient communities, centuries of tradition, spectacular wild scenery and a people whose friendliness belies the hard life that the terrain imposes on them. It is also a world of charm and treasures that is of no less beauty than its more glamorous coastal neighbours. Between San Remo and the French border there are, perhaps, no more than seven or eight roads that lead into this landscape inland from the western Riviera, the *Riviera dei Fiori* or 'Riviera of Flowers'.

Our base is in a holiday apartment in the tiny hilltop community of Perinaldo, twelve kilometres from the coastal town of Bordeghera which we can see away in the distance some six hundred metres down the valley. In daylight, the blue of the Mediterranean twinkles at us from the eyrie; at night, the bright lights of the town are a terrestrial counterpoint to the twinkling stars above.

The celestial display gives tiny Perinaldo its principal claim to fame. With an atmosphere untainted by pollution, and mountain-high winds that dissuade clouds from tarrying, the little town enjoys some of the clearest views of the region, including those heavenward.

Two hundred years ago, a local villager with an eye for the stars first appreciated these climatic conditions and thus founded a family dynasty that was to transform the world's understanding of other worlds. That Gian Domenico Cassini would achieve such fame that his name still lives on in modern astronomy is astounding; a man raised in a remote, poor mountain village with exceptionally difficult access (in those early days) to the knowledge of Genoa or other big university cities, he nevertheless made discoveries that still form the basis of modern astronomy.

He was the first to identify four of the seventeen moons of Saturn and divide up the rings of the planet. The method used still bears his name. He also gave his name to the modern-day Cassini-Huygens mission to Saturn and Titania.

He was, unlike many pioneers of science, a legend in his own time as his reputation reached out from his isolated village to the fabulous court of Louis XIV (aptly know as the Sun King).

Today his legacy, and that of the three generations of family astronomers who followed him, lives on in the village through the observatory housed in the former Franciscan convent of San Sebastiano at the eastern end of the spine that forms Perinaldo's 'Fifth Avenue'. Guided tours of the night sky are a regular event and, as recently as the August we visited, the observatory organised an 'away-trip' to Austria for the eclipse of the moon.

Just below the town, his reputed birthplace still exists; in more violent times it was also a temporary home to Napoleon and General Massera during the Italian campaign. Beside it is the parish church of San Nicolo (the lintel above the church's right-hand door is dated 1489). On the façade of the priest's lodgings, formerly the summer residence of the Marchesi Dorea di Dolceacqua, is an old sundial built to the specifications of Cassini's grandson, the astronomer Gian Domenico Maraldi.

Perinaldo's fame came from the stars. Its lifeblood, however, is rooted in what soil it can glean from the oak and beech forests that cover the hillsides and cliffs that fall away steeply from its razorback position.

Small garden plots are carved out of the hillside. Below, down in the valleys, terraced market gardens spill down the slopes. The village, like all others on the ridges surrounding it, exists in a world of contrast—a harsh terrain with a benevolent climate.

Here, the physique of the men is fashioned by hefting heavy firewood logs up the steep, narrow, winding streets from the car parks below, not from the beach sports or exclusive body shops of the rich Riviera below. Tans are burnt into the skin by the fierce sun overhead, not the solariums or body lotions of the coast. Faces are etched and stretched by wind, sun, hard labour and winter cold—not wrinkle-smooth from face-lifts or moisturising creams.

These inland villagers are a people who have had to adapt to the land. Villages like Perinaldo are carved out of the hills and cliffs. The older sections of town are a maze of tunnelled streets, with side alleys leading out into the sunlight.

Our own apartment, owned by a Tuscan neighbour, is a vertical rabbit warren hewn from the rocky hillside below the 'main' street that winds along the ridgetop. The main entrance is on one level; the back door is three storeys above on another, higher street. The stairs from the ground floor are literally cut out of a rockface that juts into the living room. To get to guest bedrooms, visitors must all walk up through the master bedroom—great for socialising, a blow against privacy.

Again like the other villages dotted deep in or up the Maritime Alps, this is a place of work rather then pleasure. There is one small grocery store supplemented by a small weekly market. There are no supermarkets, no petrol stations, no boutiques (or clothes shops of any design), no stationery or book sellers, no kitchenware suppliers, no appliance retailers . . . There are three bars and two restaurants; the restaurants are open only for the short summer tourist season and the bars are places where local men gather for conversation, television viewing or newspaper reading. Like other towns in Italy, they rarely tickle the owner's till.

The entertainment centre of the town is the bocce court, where the local men gather at 10 each night to test their skill with the silver balls beneath overhanging trees and dim floodlights. The hard-packed dirt courts are lethal for the players. Tree roots and stones jut up from the surface while twigs and branches blown from overhanging limbs mingle with countless cigarette butts strewn across the dirt. All are obstacles that can divert perfectly placed balls. A manicured championship it is not but that does not deter the players from competing with fierce intensity, a tape at the ready to be used for scoring close points.

In this way, Perinaldo mirrors the other small isolated communities that cling to some sort of life on the ridgelines or narrow valley floors inland from the broad stretch of the Mediterranean and its beaches.

Gradually, a new economic force is drifting inland into these villages. Tourists are increasingly finding their way up the hairpin, narrow roads into the villages. They are a mixed blessing.

One night at Perinaldo's bizarrely named 'Fantasy Bar', the young bartender with the very chic, frosted-blond, waved hair described the dilemma to us. In August, the height of the season, the village's population swells from its usual six hundred inhabitants to some eighteen hundred.

'Mostly Germans,' he said.

'That's good for business, for the local economy,' I naively answered.

'No, the Germans spend all their money at the sea (the coastal resorts) during the day and only come back to sleep.'

His contempt of this German injustice was almost palpable. But he seemed delighted to learn that we were a New Zealander and an American, living in Tuscany, and sitting at his bar drinking scotches and beers. Perhaps we were the economic miracle that the Germans weren't?

From the flat concrete terrace across the narrow street from the apartment's main, lower entrance door, the view to the north is spectacular—high peaks, perhaps as much as 1500 metres, fall away to the deep ravines and carved, narrow river valleys below. It seems a wonder that people have been able to make their mark in this wild terrain. But this region has known human footprints for millions of years since Cro-Magnon man sought shelter in the caves that are etched deep into cliff faces.

Today, the villagers have a more secure footing on the landscape. In the setting sun, smoke from farmers' trimmings drifts idly on the faint breeze from the Mediterranean, olive groves and citrus orchards step down the hillsides in tiers and long, low glasshouses look like sheets of ice as they, too, flow down, always down the slopes.

As darkness falls, farmhouse lights in impossibly isolated positions twinkle like glow-worms from the tiny communities like Perinaldo that somehow cling to the ridgetop eyries.

Below us is Apricale, the 'village of the sun', that spirals up through narrow cobbled streets to the *centro storico*, old town centre, and its main piazza at the top of the slope. The piazza is one of contrasts—a pre-Renaissance drinking trough and fountain, ancient stone arches, a 13th-century bell tower over the parish church and a feudal castle complete with colourful murals of modern scenes painted by contemporary artists.

The castle—Castello della Lucertola—features hanging gardens and a soaring post-medieval bell tower, an evocative backdrop for the summer season of plays, concerts and the balun tournament (played with a special ball).

Further down the Nervia Valley towards the coast, the remarkable town of Dolceacqua lies astride the river. On the far side, the old town lies huddled below the imposing castle of the Doria family, feudal lords of the village. One of the aristocratic *palazzi* that are sprinkled through the maze of streets still bears the Doria coat of arms.

In the rugged and barren depths of Tunisia, remnants of the ancient Berber people have carved out homes in the countryside around the village Matmata—the troglodytes, or cave dwellers, of Matmata. Here in Dolceacqua's old town, the villagers have created an underground life of their own. Streets and houses are tunnelled into the rocky slopes that rise from the riverbank to the castle on its strategic hilltop. It is a tortuous maze of dark and twisting alleyways and steps, unlit by the bright sun beyond its walls. Even in the brilliant daylight of mid-afternoon, street and window lights struggle to bring illumination to the gloom. Locals walking these twisted lanes seem like scurrying rodents in some dank underworld. It is an extraordinary atmosphere that somehow creates an air of superstition, menace and mystery. Until recently, the only way to cross the river to reach this *borgo* quarter of Dolceacqua from the main road was across the beautiful little late-medieval bridge over the weir below. The 33-metre arched span is at once elegant and harmonious, an architectural masterpiece described as a 'jewel of lightness'. From the 'new side' of the river, looking to the bridge, the huddle of houses and the dominating castle, it is easy to see why the great French Impressionist Claude Monet was moved to immortalise these scenes in several paintings. If the genius of the artist brought man-made fame to the village, the beauty of the surrounding land has brought another—the reigning king of the Riviera wines, Rossèse di Dolceacqua.

And so historical, architectural, cultural, natural and man-made treasures lie scattered like sparkling jewels throughout the valleys, hillsides and sharp ridges and peaks inland from the coastal playground.

. . . Seborga, a tiny 'principality', dating back to the 10th century. More recently, the 1815 Congress of Vienna overlooked the village in its efforts to redistribute European territories in the wake of the Napoleonic wars. Today Seborga fights for its independence, with its own democratically-elected Prince (George I, a local flower-grower), its own ministers and ambassadors, passports and stamps. It also harbours hopes of producing its own currency, the 'luigino'.

. . . Pigna, with its sulphurous springs whose waters are used as an effective treatment for skin conditions.

. . . Rocchetta Nervian, famed for the historic resistance by its inhabitants in 1625 against Corsican troops fighting for the Republic of Genoa.

The stern landscape and its scattered pocket-handkerchief communities are home to more than natural and man-made beauties. The real treasure of the region is more for the soul than the heart. The people who eke a hard existence out of such an inhospitable and demanding country are among the friendliest to be found anywhere—a generous, honest, smiling and welcoming community. Our stay in Perinaldo was to provide ample confirmation as day after day we encountered the warmth of the locals.

Even before we reached our apartment we were to meet this hospitality. Nina, who is the pre- and post-visitor cleaning lady for our apartment, came down to the first parking area as you enter the village to meet us and show us the way to the apartment. We had driven from Tuscany throughout the day and had a vague notion that we would arrive about '7.15 p.m.'. In the event we were perhaps fifteen minutes late and who knows how long Nina had been waiting to greet and guide us.

After introducing us to the house, she took us through the winding streets to the town's only grocery store so we would know where to go to survive.

The next day, she explained, was Perinaldo's market day, held each Wednesday in the middle of the three modest piazzas that link the main street as it runs along its ridgeline.

'You must try the chicken there. It is the best I have ever tasted anywhere,' said an accented voice in English behind us. This was Karen, the (ironically) German artist who had lived here in an apartment on the main street for fourteen years. 'It's a beautiful place to be inspired,' she assured us. We had to go to the market early in the morning before the stall owner had fired up his rotisserie, place an order, then return in the late morning to pick it up.

'That's pretty smart,' observed Nancy. 'You know how many orders you've got before you start cooking, so there's no wastage.'

The market was a remarkably good one for such a small, remote, almost inaccessible village like Perinaldo—two fruit and vegetable stalls, a delicatessen, a clothes stall and the butcher where we ordered our chicken. In a town that boasts no deli, no butcher and no clothes shops, this weekly market is an important event in the life of Perinaldo and throughout the morning drew a goodly proportion of the inhabitants to shop, meet friends or just sit on the surrounding stone benches and steps to watch the bustle of the day. In this way, Perinaldo's weekly market day was a mirror image of those that come to the towns and villages that surround us in southern Tuscany.

Even before we ventured to market on that first morning, we were greeted by a passing Italian as we sat on the terrace admiring the view and our morning coffee.

Giacomo was an 82-year-old, walrus-moustached local who

used to tend the flowers in the raised stone-and-concrete boxes set into the low wall that surrounds the terrace. He walked with a brown wooden walking cane that glowed with use. He also had a wicked sense of humour.

In retirement, he busies himself with a lovingly tended garden—a small patch of level ground just metres from our apartment—and carving statues from the wood of the olive trees that compete for space with the chestnuts and pines covering the surrounding countryside.

Most of these creations are kept in his home, perhaps twenty metres further up our narrow street. But one, he told us, had been banished by his wife to permanent exile in his workshed.

He told us it depicted two lovers and when his wife saw the completed masterpiece, she ordered, '*Vai,*' 'Go.' Giacomo laughed uproariously at the memory, bending over with mirth and banging his cane on the stone wall with delight at the story.

Later, he took me to his workshed to show me. It was not surprising that his wife had exiled the sculpture as it showed a man and a woman in a very compromising position—a most unlikely scene for an octogenarian to have created. After the 'showing' he cut roses from his garden for Nancy. And throughout our stay he would stop for a chat each morning or evening as we sat on our terrace; one day he invited us to his home to see some more of his carvings (unsurprisingly, less risqué then the workshed-consigned article) and we met his delightful wife, Rosa. As well as figurines, he made chandeliers and beautiful inlaid boxes.

One side of the terrace was defined by the walls of the apartment owned by a Frenchman with whom we came to share social greetings. At the front of the house, within a tantalising but unreachable distance from the terrace, was an apricot tree laden with ripe fruit. Each morning, as we went to the car park below, we would search the ground beneath it for fruit that had dropped but wasn't too bruised. It was frustrating—too far to reach from the terrace, too high above the car park—and he didn't seem to be eating them anyway.

But on the morning he was due to return to France, he knocked on the door and presented us with a grape-leaf-lined box full of luscious sweet apricots. It was a fine—and delicious—parting gift.

One night, we decided to 'have a go' at bocce on the unused, smaller, darker and even more treacherously-surfaced practice area behind the main, serious-players-only court. A villager asked if she could join in with one of the town's youngsters, Stefano; the latter was the first of an assembly line of the town's kids who would play a few rounds then be hauled off to bed by a parent, only to be replaced by another who would then be hauled off . . . When we finished, Carmen asked if we would like to play again the next night, this time with her husband Nico. Again, we had a great time and later enjoyed their hospitality and wine in their small apartment.

So for a week Nina, Giacomo and Rosa, our apricot-delivering French neighbour, Carmen and Nico and Stefano and the string of Perinaldo's kids and the other locals we met, enriched our stay in a way that scenery and picturesque villages by themselves cannot. Ligurians and Tuscans share a similar generosity of spirit and friendliness. At Perinaldo it was a nice change to be living in a village with its people rather than in the isolation of San Clemente.

Most visitors to the 'western gateway to Italy' naturally focus on the attractions of the coast where this region meets the ever-alluring Mediterranean.

It lacks the cachet, the exotic mystique of its more illustrious neighbour less than an hour's drive to the west; Bordeghera, Ventimiglia and Vallecrosia simply cannot compete with the sexy glamour of Cannes, Nice, St-Jean-Cap-Ferrat and Cap Martin.

Nor does it have the economic pulling power of a Monte Carlo to attract the world's super-rich and the fashion houses that clothe them—Gucci, Valentino, Hermes, Bulgar, Christian Dior—or the discreet international finance houses that offer them privacy and prestige: 'The Citibank, Private Bank', 'Lloyds Bank,

International Private Banking'.

Its high-rise workers' tenement blocks would not be out of place in Moscow, a world apart from the luxury hotel and apartment complexes that rise along the French Riviera above the luxury launches and yachts in the marinas below. To cross the border between Italy's Ventimiglia and France's Menton is to cross a chasm between a world of ostentatious, even arrogant, wealth and rundown poor-side-of-town seediness.

The obvious economic divide between the Côte d'Azur of the French Riviera and the self-styled *Riviera dei Fiori* of neighbouring Italy is startling and stark. Yet the Italian 'poor neighbours' have treasures of their own in those last twenty kilometres from the arts festival city of San Remo to the tunnel that emerges on the French Riviera at the seaside resort town of Menton.

Always, of course, there is the sea. And under a bright hot early summer sun, the Mediterranean sparkles and glitters on the surface of its deep blue as it stretches away to the unseen islands of Sardinia and Sicily and further still, the sands, palms and barren deserts of North Africa. The water is surprisingly warm even in June, before the blistering months of July and August have had a chance to work their magic.

It is certainly warm enough to attract crowds of swimmers and sunbathers. Some swimmers take themselves out to lie on the rock breakwaters that have been built offshore to provide calm swimming areas. Even on a still day, respectable-sized waves curl and foam and swirl around the swimmers, out of the shelter of the breakwaters. At San Remo, home of a famous international music festival early each year and a lively market in the main piazza of the old town, the beaches are sandy. But further west, towards the border, they are more likely to be rocky and pebbly.

Each town has its historic old centre perched atop the promontories that reach out into the water, separating the bays, coves and beaches along the coastline. Most also have an old port where local fishermen set out in stretched dinghies with nets or pots or in larger trawlers to farm the deeper waters. With the advent and ease of modern mass tourism, new marinas filled with gleaming pleasure craft sit alongside the old working port.

In the evening, tourists roaming the cobbled narrow streets might stop to dine on that day's catch—perhaps *seppie allo scoglio di zimino* (a cuttlefish dish), *polpo all'inferno* (octopus seared over open flames) or salt cod toasted on the hot stone base of the oven, flaked, mixed with boiled white beans and dressed with mild chili peppers in vinegar and olive oil.

Another local seafood speciality is the strong-tasting salted sardines in oil. As everywhere in Italy, olive oil is one of the most important ingredients in the many regional cuisines. Here on the Riviera it is almost the sole dressing used, a light pure oil from the crushed taggiasca olives which are a small, fleshy, black variety with tiny stones. This variety also produces *spremuta d'oliva*, an olive juice rich with healthy goodness.

Away from the old town and protected ports, wide promenades stretch for kilometres above the beaches. Bars, cafés, restaurants and trattorias line them, jutting out over the beach below so customers on their decks have clear views over the sea. Many have their own deck-chaired private sections of beach where customers can pay for the privilege of dining, drinking, sunbathing or swimming.

At Ventimiglia, Italy's last town before the border with France, there are the remains of an old Roman arena, testifying to its importance when Imperial Rome ruled the Mediterranean. The first level of steps, the *porta di Provenza* (gate to Provence), insulae and domus, baths and mosaic floors are still intact.

High above the new town on the side of the river Roia which bisects old Ventimiglia from the more modern commercial centre sits medieval Ventimiglia with its narrow, cobbled streets, steep alleyways, covered passageways, stone houses and archivolts—a mirror of many of the old villages of Liguria. On the far, French side of this 16th century old town is the isolated church of San Michele. The vault of its crypt is supported by granite columns; one is an old Roman milestone and another two are reputed to come from the remains of an ancient temple dedicated to Castor and Pollux. Modern Ventimiglia is a bustling centre that each

Friday swarms with thousands of locals and visitors at its weekly market stretching along the banks of the river down to the beach and into the town streets. It is said to be the largest market in Italy, if not Europe, and is a brightly covered warren of hundreds of stalls selling clothing, cooking utensils, tablecloths, leather bags and belts, specialty foods like cheeses, music, craftware, silk ties and scarves.

Thousands of people pour into the town on market day from Ventimiglia itself, from the Italian coastal towns and inland villages, and the majority of visitors from across the border in France. The stall holders are equally conversant in Italian and French (many also speak English) and switch effortlessly from Italian lire to French francs, giving change in either currency from large wads in separate money belts.

Ventimiglia also offers two entertaining diversions each year. In July, there is the 'Battle of the Flowers' with its intricately designed, highly detailed parade of floats built afresh each year by the townspeople. These enormous floats might feature beautifully patterned tropical fish, effigies of impish court jesters or even jousting knights atop charging steeds—all coated with a rainbow of bright flower petals. A month later the town also buzzes with the festival of medieval August, a series of keenly contested trials and tournaments between the *sestrieri*, or quarters of the town.

Perhaps ten kilometres further into Italy, Bordeghera has a strong connection with faraway England, rather than the French connection of Ventimiglia and its market.

It was first 'discovered' by English tourists in the late 1800s; at times during the 'season', these long-term holidaymakers even outnumbered the locals. They brought with them a passion for tennis, so much so that they persuaded the town authorities in 1878 to build Italy's first tennis club—a foreign part that is forever England.

Ten years later, as his fellow countrymen and women lobbed, ducked and dived around their courts, the English scholar Clarence Bicknill founded the museum of Ligurian palaeontology which now bears his name. The extensive collection includes impressions of stone carvings from the slopes of Mount Bego, high in the Maritime Alps that provide a rugged backdrop to the coastal Riviera. There is also an international library with over twenty thousand volumes as well as the International Institute of Ligurian Studies.

The English connection goes further; the town has something of a reputation for English-style humour and has even adopted a slogan for itself: 'Bordeghera—*Città dell'Umorismo*', 'Bordeghera —City of Humour'. Each September, it hosts an International Festival of Humour. The stamp of the British Empire has also left its impression elsewhere on this coast. On the short clifftop drive between Ventimiglia and the border, the Hanbury Gardens sweep down the promontory of Mortola to the sea below. The gardens were begun in the late 1860s by Thomas Hanbury, a landowner who made his fortune in Shanghai before falling in love with this part of the Italian Riviera and its climate.

Here, typically Mediterranean flora mingles with a host of more exotic species, forming a wonderful garden for some 6000 plants, all grown in the open air, all catalogued and marked. Every possible variety of pine and olives mix with shrubs like myrtle, laurel, rosemary and broom. By a stream grow oleanders. Shaded areas are festooned with wisteria and lilac; at the foot of walls are passion-flowers and roses, ivy and begonias; tumbling geraniums and pelargoniums cascade over terraces; there are agaves, aloes, opuntia, cacti, cereus; spurges and yuccas spread over the south-facing part of the garden.

The Hanbury family created a palm grove, an Australian eucalyptus forest and even colour-themed gardens (pink, white, orange) for seasonal colour. An orchard and citrus plantation were positioned amidst beds of anemones, freesias, irises, crocuses, jonquils and squills.

Each tier of the stepped garden as it flows down the hillside was enhanced by sculptures, fountains, tubs, colonnades and pillars, amphorae, stone seats and small temples. The Hanbury villa, halfway down the slope, is a handsome *palazzo* of coppery stucco with a distinctive square tower to enhance the view over the sea and the coastline to the east. Large raised terraces sit on each side and an arched loggia and portico greets visitors to the front entrance. The visionary Thomas Hanbury lived only a further eight years after buying the 18-hectare property. But his family continued his dream of creating a unique botanical park. Today, he and his wife are buried side by side beneath a tall open-sided pergola amidst the plants, trees, shrubs and flowers he envisioned. The gardens now belong to the people of Italy and are administered and maintained by the Botanical Institute of the University of Genoa; the legacy of Thomas Hanbury and his family is studied by leading botanical scientists and admired by thousands of visitors each year.

A totally different—and quite curious—attraction lies a little to the east where the twin towns of new (coastal) Vallecrosia spreads up a valley to the smaller village of Old Vallecrosia, perhaps some two kilometres inland. Here, amidst seedy garden sheds and weed-strewn patches of empty land, proudly sits the Museum of Italian Song, housed incongruously on a riverbank in an old steam locomotive and carriages. It is a bizarre sight and an even more bizarre site.

For train buffs, the steam engine is the 'cirilla', an '835-157' tender, serial number 83657, with three double axles. Twenty-three of these were produced in 1910 by Officine Mecchaniche di Milano. The museum display itself is housed in a number of connected carriages (literally 'one hundred doors') which were used by the Italian State Railways until the 1970s.

Spiral staircases and wrought iron balconies have been added to the engine, reportedly to enhance its appearance.

Inside the carriages, the functional wooden seats, luggage compartment and lavatories have been removed to make way for rooms with 'Orient Express' style furnishings, as well as display cabinets and cases. There is a history of San Remo's Italian Song Festival, displays of antique instruments, the story of the first recorded music and a collection of rare records. Quite how a Museum of Italian Music came to be established almost in the middle of nowhere up a narrow, seldom visited, valley road and to be housed in an old steam train is one of the mysteries of life. To be sure, there is more to Italian music than opera, but opera is such a dominant and famed part of Italian culture that one would imagine such a museum would be better housed—and better appreciated—in some magnificent palazzo in a centre of opera like Milan or Naples. But it seems that some Vallecrosian train-spotting enthusiast with a passion for music dreamt up the concept first and, presto, here lies the Museum of Italian Music.

As long as a million years ago the early ancestors of present-day inhabitants strode this coastline. Cro-Magnon man lived in deep caves by the sea beneath the sheer cliffs below the tiny village of Grimaldi, the last settlement before the French border. The caves of Balzi Rossi ('Red Crags', after the rugged terrain of the area and the reddish colour of the rocks) were a home and a refuge for these prehistoric forebears. They hunted, fished, did stonework and made bone or teeth necklaces before disappearing leaving mystery behind them, but also remnants of their passage in the form of members of the *razza dei Grimaldi*, or Grimaldi race, distinguished by their markedly Negroid features, as well as the skeletons of several men and a young woman buried with full funeral honours. Later, some two hundred thousand years ago, these same caves became a home for *Homo erectus*.

Excavation work by archaeologists has uncovered a large number of finds in the deep caves and vertical crevices of the cliffs. Many are now housed in Italy's National Museum of Prehistory—complex stone tools, soapstone statuettes or Venuses (stylised figures of women used as symbols of fertility) and a unique depiction of the Prewaskrii horse, carved from rock by a hunter-cum-artist some 20,000 years ago. The caves have also revealed evidence of the severe climate changes over the millennia—fossils of elephants, hippopotami, and rhinoceroses reflecting hot ages, and of marmots and reindeer testifying to the cold or ice ages that froze this part of Italy which today boasts palm trees, semi-tropical flowers, citrus and fruit trees, warm seas and hot sun.

Ten

Of Michelangelo, marble and mosaic

$\mathcal{A}$LMOST exactly five hundred years ago, a morose young man sat confronting a physical and mental dilemma. There was little need for his moroseness. He was, at twenty-six years, in his prime. He had talent. He had fame. He had the patronage of the wealthy. And he was living at a time of great endeavours.

Artists like Raphael and Cellini were creating their masterpieces. Another, Leonardo da Vinci, was devising not only great artworks but also revolutionary inventions that would not be realised for those five hundred years—devices like the helicopter. A young noble, thin and almost feminine, had just returned from studies in France that would help give him a name that still stalks the political stages of the world—Niccolò Macchiavelli.

This was the time of the rebirth, the renewal of a continent, of faith in the nobility and creativity of humankind. And our morose young man was to be its major spokesman.

His name was Michelangelo. That we know. We also know

he was an ill-tempered young man. We know his father was of noble stock but had fallen on hard times, the family making do in an isolated little village in mountains far removed from the splendours of Rome and Siena and Florence, where he now sat. He had a contradictory personality. His personal habits were described as 'repulsive' and, on instruction from his father, he never washed. Yet he desired property and rejected the merits of other artists who 'want to ruin me'. Raphael was dismissed with disdain: 'all he had in art he had of me'.

We know he hated his city and its people. 'I never had to do with a more ungrateful and arrogant people than the Florentines,' he would write. That was a rather ungrateful sentiment in itself, considering the largesse the powerful patron of the city was to give him. And we know that the great block of stone presenting him with a dilemma this day had already defeated artists like da Vinci. It was an imposing presence and presented massive problems. Five metres tall, it weighed many tonnes. It was woven through with cracks that threatened its integrity and strength. It had been marred by the attempts of others to make something of it. Called *Il Gigante*, the Giant, it had been carved from high on a mountain forty years before, lowered with an ancient system of logs and ropes to the coastal plain below, hauled by oxen to the port some seven kilometres away, loaded on a ship, carried down the coast and up a river called the Arno to the great centre of Florence.

And now the young Michelangelo had been commissioned to create from it a statue to demonstrate the values of the Republic of Florence and its liberty from the twin tyrannies of foreign rule and papal domination—an 'heroic conception of the human will'.

But how to represent such a grand theme? How to capture and draw such an essence from this great slab of stone? He had already created one majestic masterpiece; it was called the *Pietà*. Other glories still lay within him—the dome of St Peter's Cathedral in Rome, the Last Judgement of its Sistine Chapel, the Bacchus of Florence's Bargello museum . . . .

Three years later, his work was finished. He called it *David*.

Such a simple idea, such a simple image, such a simple concept. But what a powerful one! Even the people of the day recognised his genius. Fully thirty leading artists of the time—da Vinci, Botticelli, Lippi among them—were charged with selecting a site to display the masterpiece. Finally, a decision was made to place it in one of Florence's signature locations, the Piazza della Signoria. Over the years its broad expanse has served as an arena for spectacles, political gatherings, public executions and other such events. The small Piazza san Giovanni that separates the towering face of the famous Duomo Cathedral from its *battistero*, baptistery, has long been Florence's spiritual heart. The Piazza della Signoria has been its temporal one. In winter, it is a bleak, forlorn stone lawn of dark misery; in summer, it is a sea of tourists who come to see its statues, arches, old buildings and the Uffizi art gallery. Many like to sit in the summer heat at one of the pretentious cafés that face on to it. For the privilege they will pay outrageous prices for refreshments.

It took four days to wheel the incarnated *Gigante* into its home from the Duomo workshop where it had been those three years in the making.

There it stood for three hundred and seventy years until the brutality of the city's winter climate and heat of its summer forced it indoors to its current home, the Accademia, the first such academy dedicated to the arts in Europe. How many of those video-camera-toting tourists in the Piazza della Signoria realise the David they are capturing for the folks back home is a replica made in 1873?

But that lay in the future. Now, in 1501, Michelangelo had to consider the huge stone before him. Science knows it as calcium carbonate. He knew it as *marmo*. In English, we call it marble. It is not a particularly rare material; it is found in many parts of the world. But it has two qualities that have made it a prized stone for centuries. It has durability, which makes it ideal for outdoor use. And it has nobility, which can be transformed into great beauty.

Tuscany has given many treasures to Italy and the world: great artists like Michelangelo, Dante and Donatello; the Renaissance; the beauty of its landscape; the glorious cities and towns like Florence, Siena, Pienza; the Italian language itself. And it has given a mountain, literally, of the finest marble.

But only just. The jagged mountain sits behind Carrara, the last northern Tuscan town before you pass into the province of Liguria. From Trequanda it is an easy three-hour drive, less if you time it to miss the traffic on the motorway where it loops around the southern and western edges of Florence. From Florence, you head west, towards the town famous for its leaning tower and the Mediterranean coastline. The motorway here, too, skirts Pisa and turns right to the north through the coastal plain between the sea and the daunting Apuan Alps inland. Carrara, the town that gives its name to the stone that gives it its wealth, sits in the foothills of this steep and rugged range. It is, perhaps, ten kilometres inland from the sea. From its elevated streets the blue is tantalisingly close, a sweet promise of sun and sand.

Carrara is to marble as Nepal is to Mt Everest, as Lapland is to reindeer, as Florida is to the Everglades. The two are indistinguishable. The town even takes it name from the marble mountain behind it—*kar* is an Indo-European word for stone. (The Italians have to bow to the Greeks for the origin of the word marble, *marmaros*.)

Even before you reach the town, a ceaseless caravan of open-backed trucks passes, heading for the port at the coast or into the cities of Europe. Each is laden with a huge block of marble on its tray. Throughout our visit to Carrara, this cavalcade from the quarries never stopped—one, two, three, more trucks a minute.

Driving into town you pass countless shops, yards filled with blocks of marble or piled with the leftovers from worked blocks. Some are mere backyard sheds, some substantial factories. From them, the screeches of diamond-tipped cutting saws swirl out to mix with the roar of the truck convoy.

In the town itself, the streets are not paved with gold but with marble—literally. We walked by one street where workmen were paving a footpath with marble slabs. Building façades, statues, terraces, balustrades, stairways—all are marble. Whites, browns, greens, blacks, greys, mottled. Marble even finds its way into the toilets. I had to make a visit to the gents in a bar where we had lunch. It was one of those hole-in-the-floor affairs that you can still encounter in Italy. The hand-basin was porcelain, but the place where you stood and the two raised feet you used were marble. It seemed somewhat excessive.

But there is a downside, a trade-off. If you live at the beach you have to expect sand. After great windstorms in the Sahara, we would even get coatings in Trequanda—a thousand and more kilometres away and in the middle of the Italian countryside.

In Carrara, it is dust. White dust. A cloud of white that you cannot see in the air but you find coating everything. Leave your car for a few minutes and it takes on a ghostly air. Walk the streets and leave white footprints on the car's carpet. It is insidious. To be a housewife, a butcher or a restaurant owner in Carrara must be a miserable career, a non-stop task of wiping, dusting, cleaning and vacuuming. It comes sweeping out from the workshops, propelled by wind or the power of the machines sawing and sanding. It blows from the slabs on the trucks as they pass through the town. But above all it comes down from the marble mountain behind the town, a white-cloaking revenge on the town that attacks it with such rapacity.

From the north-south autostrada along the coast, the scars of centuries are clearly visible against the grey of the surrounding peaks that have not been assaulted. The mountains are austere with little relieving vegetation to give them colour. At this distance, you can discern the white of the exposed marble. It's not a brilliant, snowfield white—the surrounding grey muddies it. But as you drive inland towards the town, the white intensifies and you begin to understand why Carrara marble has seduced artists, rulers and architects. Marble comes in many guises, both in colours and purities. The snow-white marble from here is ninety-nine per cent pure. You have to walk in the town to understand how the mountain owns it economically. But before then, as you reach the outskirts, you understand how it owns it physically. It is an all-imposing, physical presence rearing over the buildings below, nearly two thousand metres at its peak height. It is not a picture postcard mountain; the scars have destroyed its scenic qualities. It has an angry air about it. And a challenging one: take me on if you dare.

For two thousands years, men have been doing just that. They have had to endure the harshest conditions, risk injury and death, devise ingenious excavation methods and construct intricate transport systems. The story of Carrara marble is as much a triumph of courage and engineering as it is of beauty and artistry.

The results can be admired today around the world, not only in Michelangelo's *David* and *Pietà*.

The Imperial Romans were the first to use it to celebrate power and empire—the Temple of Apollo on Rome's Palatine Hill, Trajan's Column, Cesto's Pyramid, Constantine's Colosseum, the Portico of Ottavia, the Arches of Titus and Septimis Severus were created using Carrara marble. The emperor Augustus redecorated Rome in part with it. It was used on the façade of Florence's great Duomo. The noble palaces and gardens of Europe were built from it and then decorated with statues and monuments of the marble from the mountain. Jean-Antoine Houdon's statue of George Washington was created using it.

It has always attracted the great stone-working artists. But other artists with different but no less great talent have been drawn too by the mountain and the mystique of its stone—Dickens and Tolstoy are but two who have witnessed the carving of the blocks from the mountain. Up close it is a thrilling experience. It is also a humbling one.

Today, there are some ninety working quarries, or *cave*, exploiting the cubic kilometres of marble the mountain holds. They are located in three huge excavation areas. The most obvious quarries are the opencast ones. They rise—vertically, it seems—for hundreds of metres. They are like great gashes on the face of the mountain, as if some giant has used a huge hunting knife to slice down into the 'meat' of the mountain and then ripped it apart. Onto the cliff faces have been carved zigzag roads (a kind word to describe them; wide goat trails might be better) for the endless stream of trucks ascending, empty, to the quarry face where the enormous blocks are loaded on so the trucks can return. Then there are the wall quarries that cut into the face, creating amphitheatres with curtains of marble as a backdrop. Finally, there are the mine quarries that tunnel deep into the mountain where giant cathedrals are created.

To reach them is an easy matter in a vehicle, a short drive of perhaps twenty or thirty minutes up the sealed road leading out of the town. It's a steep and winding road, so narrow that in places you might have to pull over and stop for an approaching tour coach (and there are plenty of them). But it is by no means a difficult one. It passes through forests and past, naturally, marble workshops as well as small communities, bars, shops and isolated houses before you open out onto the bare landscape of the mountain. It is difficult to imagine how, before the coming of the road and even a freight railway, earlier workmen managed to create a marble industry at all. How did the first quarriers, the Romans, hack accessways up the steep mountain, through the forests and then into the hard rock? How did they negotiate the plunging ravines and vertical rock walls? How did they get the implements and tools they needed up there for the carts and oxen? Even more remarkable, how did they bring those enormous and heavy blocks down the mountainside?

We know that the early Romans used slaves to do the heavy work (one of the three excavation areas, Colonnata, is said to have been named after columns of slaves marching up to misery). Poor souls were brought from their distant homes to live a life whose harshness we can only shudder at. But even they needed access routes, tools, transport equipment, overseers, guards . . .

What a hellish world it must have been; the cruel cold of winter; the oven of summer when the Tuscan sun glared back from the rock face; the aching bodies after a day of unremitting hard labour; perhaps the sting of the overseer's whip; no doubt the ceaseless hunger from a miserable ration of food; the loneliness of separation from homeland and home.

And always the danger.

The marble mountain is a mistress of death. It takes no imagination, standing before these sheer cliffs and seeing the great stones, to understand that injury and death are constants in the lives of those who work here. No one knows how many lives have been lost over the centuries to bring such joy to the world. Certainly it must be thousands.

In other times, the quarries were pretty much left to run themselves—privately managed arenas of death where marble-hungry owners were more concerned with raping the mountain to feed a world rather than protecting their workers.

The injury and mortality rate reached such proportions that the local *commune*, the town council, was forced to step in. It now licences private companies or co-operatives that work the quarries (cynics might suggest that it's another great way to gather tax revenue). For a yearly fee, this gives them the right to quarry the stone. But they also have to adhere to rules governing such issues as worker safety and the environment. If not, the licences can be revoked.

However, despite any attempts to improve working conditions, this will always be a dangerous place. Three ambulances stationed outside the offices of a centrally located quarry are a silent reminder of this.

Over the years, new technologies have been developed or incorporated into the quarrying to increase efficiency in both excavating and transporting. Wooden wedges, wire saws, even dynamite for a time—but that proved more dangerous for both men and marble. An ancient manual system known as *lizzatura* used ropes and logs to bring the blocks down on soaped paths, then onto bullock-powered carts and, finally, onto a railway system carved through the mountain.

Today, a new technology brought into use just a few decades ago has dramatically increased that long-sought efficiency. Before the diamond saw, the marble could only be cut at a rate of about five centimetres a day. Now the rate is up to twenty centimetres *an hour*.

Such a quantum leap in productivity means some 1.5 million tonnes of stone are now cut from the marble mountain each year. Another two million tonnes are removed to be used as calcium carbonate for industrial purposes. And such is the skill of the townspeople who work these prodigious quantities that another two million tonnes of marble and granite are shipped each year to Carrara from around the world.

The fascination with this stone seems unquenchable. In its raw state, freshly carved from the mountain, it sparkles and its crystalline structure is evident by its sandpapery feel. But worked and polished, it is transformed into a glistening material with the sleek smoothness of satin. It is little wonder that kings and nobles and emperors have sought it as a token of wealth and status over the centuries. Even modern-day would-be emperors have looked to Carrara to provide symbols of their power.

The longest block ever carved from the mountain was ordered by Rome's new emperor in the 1920s. Mussolini, Il Duce, wanted a symbol of ancient Rome to represent his modern empire, fascism. The block—some nineteen metres long, 2.35 metres high and 2.35 metres wide—was excavated in January 1929, from the Carbonera quarry in the Fantiscritti basin, one of the three great excavation areas eight hundred metres up the mountain. It weighed three hundred tonnes. It was obviously going to be a feat of some magnitude to bring it down the mountain. In fact it took eight months to bring it down and then take it to the dock across the coastal plain.

Reputedly, the workers, authorities and drafted-in police used for the job employed some seventy thousand litres of soap to grease the way down and twenty-five large iron ropes. In Carrara it was encased in a cage that needed fifty tonnes of wood and fourteen tonnes of iron. Thirty-six pairs of oxen then hauled it to the docks.

Today, it stands as an obelisk in Rome's Foro Italico, an ironic tribute to a discredited political regime and its arrogant leader. No doubt it will be there for another two or more millennia after its creator's bullet-ridden corpse was hung by its heels in a symbolic gesture of the end of his dream of a new Roman empire.

It would be easy to dismiss Il Duce's dreams of grandeur as an arrogant folly. But that would be churlish. For at least in selecting his great memorial, he recognised the power and beauty—the nobility—of the marble. In that he was in the company of real emperors and the great artists like Michelangelo. In Carrara, they found a mountain of marble from which to carve their legacies to the world.

Even in death, Michelangelo rules Florence. As you drive down the Viale Galileo Galilei, the city and its artery, the river Arno, open out before you on the valley floor. Halfway down, you can park in the open space of the Piazzale Michelangelo. You won't be alone. Here, tour buses release their hordes to mill around the souvenir stalls and have their photograph taken at the wall overlooking the city below. There was even a Japanese wedding party at the restaurant on the terrace below one day. It is not so much a piazza as a car park to lure the coaches. Tacky souvenir stalls complete the picture.

But the view is magnificent. The sullen dark of the Arno, the shop-cluttered arches of the Ponte Vecchio, the famous Boboli gardens to the left.

Three sights dominate the eye: the immense domed majesty of the Duomo, the cathedral; the prim square tower of the Uffizi, the town hall; and the stolid, brooding bulk of the 13th century Santa Croce.

For me, Florence's Bargello is superior as a repository of art to the more famous Uffizi a block away. Its Cellini sculptures in particular are sublime. And—here's that man again—Michelangelo's statues of Bacchus and Brutus are studies in power.

Santa Croce holds more fascination than the Duomo. Not for the outside; a stiff, pragmatic building, it lacks the ability to catch the breath that its more illustrious, domed 'competitor' a ten-minute walk away has. It imposes itself on the skyline, rather than enhancing it.

Perhaps that reflects the fancies of the reputed founders of the church. Saint Francis of Assisi is said to have personally founded the first Santa Croce church on the site. Presumably he would have been irritated if not incensed by what now stands as he was a believer in devotional modesty 'for they ought not to raise great churches for the sake of preaching to the people or for any other reason, for they will show greater humility and give a better example by going to preach in other churches'.

But competition is competition and the religious marketplace is as fierce in finding new customers as any. Faced with competing orders like the Dominicans, then embarking on construction of the equally dominant Santa Maria Novella on the other, western, side of town, the proponents of the new Santa Croce were not going to be outdone. They were Franciscans, by God, and they'd have the biggest and best church in their neck of the woods. The fact that they represented a religious order that championed poverty was, apparently, irrelevant. They were happy to embrace excess—and fortunes were ploughed into the building by rich families hoping some of their consciences would be soothed by giving to this 'humble' fraternity.

The order also embraced other excesses. Their rival Dominicans held the local Inquisition franchise until 1254, when these pious and loving Franciscans decided they'd like the job. The Head Inquisitor set up shop in Santa Croce and sent forth his brothers—two armed friars and a lawyer—to seek out heretics. With a few cute little tricks of the trade, they could get a confession quicker than the Republicans can rig a Florida election. Perhaps they had apprenticeships or night schools in 'Torture: The Religious Imperative and Practical Techniques' or 'Rack Design' or 'The Iron Maiden and its efficient use'.

These Inquisitors were certainly masters of their trade. The historic medieval town of San Gimignano lies in the hills about equidistant between Florence and its traditional rival to the south, Siena. It is principally noted for the towers that once dominated its skyline and gave it its nickname of the 'medieval Manhattan'. At one time, more than seventy were crammed behind its walls; today a mere fifteen remain. Apart from its beauty as a hilltop town, it offers the many thousands of tourists who 'discover' it each year a number of fresco cycles, some rather risqué for the period they were painted—the 'Wedding Scene' frescos from the 14th century, for example, depict a wife riding astride her husband's back and a couple sharing a bath. It seems unlikely they were following an environmentalist's dictum to save water.

Another fresco cycle, in San Gimignano's old cathedral, the Collegiata, has a more wholesome subject—episodes from the life of Santa Fina, one of the town's most adored saints. After St Gregory appeared in a vision foretelling her impending death, Santa Fina retired to a wooden board for five years to await it. Such steadfastness did not, however, restrict her miracle-working. From her five-year death-board she is said to have busied herself with such matters as restoring sight to a choirboy, healing the paralysed hand of her nurse and bringing down angels to ring the cathedral bells. Her good works were obviously well received; when she (finally) expired, flowers sprouted from her board and from one of the town's towers.

A short walk from the Collegiata, across the central piazza with its old well and down the street opposite, is a reminder of the glories of the church as it went about its work. Behind a modest entrance way is San Gimignano's latest contribution to Tuscan culture—a museum, dedicated to torture. Here you can learn how man through the centuries has perfected ways to put his fellows through a perverted hell. There are examples, naturally, of the Iron Maiden, that upright cupboard inlaid with fearsome metal spikes to impale the hapless victim sitting inside. You can admire the neat symmetry and clever ingenuity of the rack. The guide book to the museum and its implements carries a number of paintings showing the various techniques and implements man devised to improve his ability to wreak pain and havoc on his fellows. One lingers in the mind: a poor soul is strung up in mid-air by his ankles, legs pulled apart. On a specially erected platform, front and rear of the suspended victim, two men busy themselves sawing down from the man's crotch in much the same way as loggers would use a sawpit to produce planks, or as the old miners sawed marble with a wire.

Not surprisingly, many of the devices and practices were developed during the Inquisition. Given the fever that that dark period induced, perhaps it is not surprising that the peace-loving, poverty-espousing Franciscans embraced such cruelty as they set out on their daily heretic hunt through the dark, narrow streets of Florence.

It is bitter irony that Santa Croce, a building dedicated to God, was a headquarters of hell. The citizens of the city must have regarded it with terror rather then piety, and who could blame them?

And so, with a brief afternoon detour to San Gimignano, we find ourselves back on the cobblestones of the Piazza Santa Croce, downtown Florence. And it is literally downtown. This is the city's lowest point, as was proven so dramatically and disastrously in the great flood of 1966. It was an event of Biblical proportions, triggered by forty days of continuous rain. Over the years, the city has experienced many floods when the Arno has burst its banks—1269, 1333, 1557, 1884. Its ability to create havoc belies Mark Twain's caustic dismissal of this 'great historical creek with four feet of water in the channel . . . would be a very plausible river, if they would pump some water into it.'

In summer, it's a fair assessment as the same torpor that sets over the city (tourists excluded) infects the river as it lackadaisically struggles between its high embankments, its surface broken only by training rowers and lazy ducks.

But on the morning of 4 November 1966, its latent power was released, fuelled by those forty days of rain including forty-eight centimetres in the preceding two days alone. Finally, enough was enough for the land to absorb and a great wall of mud and water thundered through the city in the pre-dawn gloom. It was the power of nature at its most brutal.

The carnage was enormous: thirty-five dead, hundreds of homes and thousands of cars destroyed, buildings like Santa Croce awash with six metres of water. On a human scale, it was a great tragedy. But on an artistic one it was worse.

The surging water ripped five of the famous Ghiberti panels from the doors of the Baptistery, opposite the Duomo. They were recovered some two kilometres away. The cellars of the Uffizi, housing thousands of precious paintings, were filled with mud. Some 1.5 million books in the Biblioteca Nazionale were damaged—two-thirds of them beyond repair. Indeed, restoration of paintings, books and other art treasure continues today; eighty full-time staff still work on the damaged volumes from the library. Two-thirds of the three thousand paintings and sculptures recovered from the flood's slurry are now back on display to the public.

An enduring emblem of the disastrous flood was the sight of the famous *Crucifix* painting by the so-called father of Italian art, Cimabue, as it was carried away by the water. In 1971, on the fifth anniversary of the devastation, Florence's mayor rather floridly wrote: 'When Cimabue's *Crucifix* was carried past, fatally wounded . . . even the most hardened men, the loudest blasphemers, stopped in their muddy labours and took off their hats in silence; every woman, no matter how tough or dishonest, crossed herself with sincerity . . . It was as still and silent as on Good Friday.'

Perhaps I am too harsh describing Signor Bargellini's evocation as florid. The flood was a cathartic moment in Florence's never-dull history and the passions unleashed are understandable. Fortunately, the *Crucifix* was not 'fatally wounded'. Like the Baptistery doors it was recovered and, although too damaged to restore to its original state, now resides in Santa Croce's Refectory.

If the church was once a headquarters of terror, it is now a treasure-house of beauty. Frescos by Giotto, the pupil who outdid his discoverer and teacher Cimabue, and great tombs and monuments to some of the most important people of history are within its cavernous interior. There is the tomb of Galileo, the physicist, astronomer and mathematician generally acknowledged to be the first modern scientist. Dante's association with Florence is also recognised by the large statue outside the building and the monument inside. Macchiavelli reposes here. Amidst the angels and Madonnas there is a monument to a more modern angel of mercy, Florence Nightingale, who was born in the city in 1820 and named after it. And then there is the tomb of Michelangelo, sculptor of marble; he claimed his genius with working the stone came from the marble dust he swallowed in the milk of his wet-nurse, who came from Carrara. His tomb is the first the visitor encounters by the left of the entrance. There is no coincidence in its location—reputedly he wanted to be buried by the entrance so the dome of the great *Duomo*—'similar to you I will not, better than you I cannot'—would be his first sight when tombs flew open on Judgement Day.

It is impossible not to be affected by Santa Croce. But don't worry, you will be in good company. Byron wrote:

In Santa Croce's holy precincts lie,
Ashes which make it holier, dust which is,
Even in itself an immortality.

There is neat symmetry about the location of Michelangelo's tomb. In the same era that he and other great sculptors were carving their reputations, another artistic stone-working tradition was emerging. Unlike the use of marble, Florence could claim this development as distinctly its own. For centuries, man has used coloured stone to create artworks, decorate homes and wear as ornamentation. The Byzantines were the first major 'school' of mosaic, the tradition of using polished stone to create pictures, motifs and patterns. They used largish (by mosaic standards) tiles. The Imperial Romans used much smaller pieces.

And that was the way of it for fifteen hundred years.

Florence and its noblest achievement—the birth of the Renaissance—are irrevocably linked to one family name, the Medicis; bankers, political weavers, providers of royal spouses and, perhaps their most enduring legacy, patrons of the arts. There are few families who have been so instrumental in reshaping the world.

Their sons and daughters provided bed- and soul-mates for rulers like Philip II of Spain, Henri II of France, Charles I of England and Mary, Queen of Scots. They became popes and cardinals, they owned an enormous financial empire, and they raised armies and razed cities. They ruled Florence, in effect if not name, for more than three centuries, no mean feat when Europe was such a fractious continent. They founded Europe's public library. They fostered the arts. And, with Lorenzo the Magnificent, they even created them. He was the perfect person in a perfect place at a perfect time; serendipity could find no finer moment. He was wealthy, powerful, educated, a poet, a diplomat and a believer in the arts who combined all these qualities to encourage them. Better still, he was alive at a time when a rare calm prevailed throughout what is today Italy and the Renaissance was at its most glorious, rejoicing in renewed values like grand architecture, noble art and a civilised way of living.

Who knows how his interest in mosaic work began? A journey to Rome where he noted that style? Or a report from a friend recently returned from the east with comments on the Byzantine tilework. Or simply a stroll along the banks of the Arno where he idly picked up a stone to skip across its surface? It does not really matter now. But we do know that we can credit him with conjuring up the notion of Florentine mosaics, of inlaying semi-precious stone to create beautiful designs.

While Lorenzo was responsible for originating the tradition, later Medici family members pursued it with such interest and vigour that, later, it is still a flourishing and prized art form, uniquely Florentine.

Working in dusty little workshops, hunched over low tables, modern Lorenzos continue to create their art; they are artists, not artisans or craftsmen. To describe them as other than this would demean the great beauty they create. The workshops are scattered across the city landscape and the tourist may find them difficult to locate. But one workshop is easy to discover. Fittingly, it is just a few metres from the tomb of the most famous of all stone-workers, Michelangelo, master of marble.

Standing in the Piazza Santa Croce in front of the building's front façade, there is a street running down the left-hand side, Via di San Guiseppe. Like most streets in the city centre, it's a narrow, cobbled affair. If you walked to the end, you would emerge by the Arno at the hectic Viale della Giovine Italia, one of Florence's frenetic main thoroughfares. But it is only a short stroll (or hop to dodge the cars and ubiquitous motor scooters that plague the city) of about fifty metres to the Arte Musiva showroom and workshops on the left, about halfway down the length of Santa Croce and on the opposite side of the street.

So it is easy to find. But it is also easy to pass it by. Only a modest little sign announces its presence. The small display window has a limited number of its products on show. In the heat of summer, the workshop door may also be open on to the street but it has a serious air about it that would dissuade all but the most gregarious from even poking their heads inside.

But for more than a century and a quarter since the first family member moved to Tuscany from native Sicily, the Sandron family has been producing stunning art from stone.

Malachite from Russia, lapis lazuli from Iran, landscape stone from Egypt, agates, alabasters, chalcedony, even lilac stone from 'uptown' Florence and *pietra paesana*, country stone, from the hills above it . . . a whole world, and a world of colour.

From these polished stones, the artists create intricate and beguiling works: tabletops, vases, landscapes, portraits, jewel caskets, armoires and chests.

Some of the more famed creations are on display in Florence's museums. The Palazzo Pitti, the ancestral home of the Medici family for two centuries, is a daunting building atop a wide flight of steps just across the Arno, on the southern side of the city. Most people get to it by jostling through the endless throngs crowding the Ponte Vecchio and the jewellery shops that dominate its passageway. Today, the best perspective of the bridge is from a distance. Hitler, it is said, saved it (but not the other bridges across the river) from destruction as the Nazis retreated. The flood of 1966 surged through it but it survived. Hopefully

21st century tourism won't cause it to buckle.

Bearing right up the easy slope of the Via dei Guicciardini brings the visitor quickly to the Piazza dei Pitti with the enormous palace façade on the left up the broad open expanse of the steps. The sight has been frowned upon by many. One description likened it to a 'rusticated Stalinist ministry'. The British writer Arnold Bennett thought it 'a rather expensive barracks'. Barracks or not, it does house some important collections. The Galleria Palatina, for example, with paintings by Raphael, Rubens, Velazquez and Titian. And in the Sala Buia are sixteen pieces of mosaic work collected by Lorenzo, including the early Byzantine and Roman forms.

It is appropriate, then, that the artform he created and collected resides in the family headquarters (the second; the first was in the Palazzo Vecchio beside the Uffizi).

Among their many other creations, the Medicis can perhaps also lay claim to what was thought a modern phenomenon—the doggy bag. Describing evenings of entertainment at the Palazzo Pitti, Anthony Trollope commented caustically of his fellow guests: 'Guests used to behave abominably. The English would seize plates of bonbons and empty the contents into their coat pockets. The ladies would do the same with their pocket handkerchiefs . . . I never saw an American pillaging . . . though I may add that American ladies would accept any amount of bonbons . . . I have seen large portions of fish, sauce and all, packed up in newspaper and deposited in a pocket. I have seen fowls and ham share the same fate, without any newspaper at all. I have seen jelly carefully wrapped in an Italian countess's lace *mouchoir* . . .'

Elsewhere in the city, other examples of the mosaic artists' work at its best can also be seen. These valuable museum pieces are untouchable. But when you enter Remo Sandron's little artistic world you can feel, sense, *experience* the effort that has gone into the works produced here.

Remo was a rather portly, moustached man in his fifties or early sixties when Nancy and I first entered his world. Like some modern Lorenzo the Magnificent, he sat behind his counting desk, or service counter. He had a slightly roguish air about him, a big sunburst of a smile and a raffish Italian charm. He also had a love of his art and was delighted to demonstrate it in practice in his workshop.

There are three rooms on the premises. The largest is the showroom, where the finished work is displayed on walls, tables, and even in desks and drawers. If we were aboard some fancy cruise liner plying the Mediterranean's chic ports, this would be the first-class passenger zone with its deck-level cabins, casino and captain's table.

At the rear and right is the engine room, where the saws and polishers power Remo's little ship. And then there are the crew quarters, the workshop, where the solutions and decisions that make this little shop run are made. This is where the artists work. Remo himself does not do the work—'I have not the patience.'

But with his excellent English, the ebullient Remo is delighted to take visitors on a tour of the premises and describe how a piece of Florentine mosaic is created. It is a wonderful, intricate, even miraculous process.

It sounds so simple: the stone arrives, cut into thin manageable pieces for handling; it is wetted or polished to reveal its colours. If the artist has a vision for an image, he selects the colours he needs; a piece of the required size and shape is cut from the stone; he glues it together; and, *voilà*, a Florentine mosaic.

The factors at play are innumerable, intertwined and endless. Michelangelo at least had his piece of Carrara stone before him as he contemplated how he should represent the 'heroic conception of human will'. It had height, breadth and width—dimension—and could be placed so he could work around it. It had one quality—marble. It had one colour—white. It was, then, a given. Without at all refuting the genius of Michelangelo or putting the artists of Remo's modest little Arte Musiva on the same elevated pedestal, consider the variables.

First, the mosaic artist must start with an image, a vision, a dream. In that, he is not alone. The painter must see his picture; the writer must have a concept. It is the creative spark that ignites the mind, drives it to depict a liquid landscape or describe a tortured soul. Then there is the stone, the materials, with which he will realise the dream. Like marble, every stone comes with different characteristics. It may be multi-hued, freckled, dappled, rippled. It may have warmth or frigidity. It may shimmer or have the depth of an ocean canyon. It may be flawed or perfect. And all those qualities may be found in a single square metre of one stone. Our artist has dozens of stones to work with, each having its own distinctions. Together, the permutations are staggering.

At an elementary level, it is like putting together a jigsaw puzzle without the aid of the picture on the top of its box; a slow process of selecting a stone, shaping it and piecing it together with the next.

Let's say our mosaic worker (for simplicity's sake, we'll call him Marco) wants to create a flower, a full, open, crimson rose. It will have shadows and tints; its petals will need shading and hues. Its leaves and stalk will have grades of green.

He may make a sketch of his rose to help keep the image in his mind. Then he will go into the studio's engine room to begin selecting his stone. It's a small, dim room where the cutting and polishing is done. Dust from years of this work coats the floors and shelves.

The stone has already been cut thin to reveal its internal colouring, which helps Marco select his colours without the waste of ruining a piece of uncut stone. Slabs lie stacked against a wall, smaller pieces from those already used rest on shelves. Offcut fragments, also still usable, are stored sway in drawers.

For ease of handling, the bigger slabs are cut into smaller pieces. The power saw used for this work is a machine that Heath Robinson might proudly have designed—a cranky, clanky old affair resplendent with big belts, like those old foot-pedal sewing machines your grandmother plied in her drawing room. It might, in fact, have been produced around the time Remo's family first established themselves in Florence. 'In the old times, we used sand friction [for the cutting]; now is [C]arborundum,' he explained.

From this piece Marco must then select the fragment he needs—the right colour, the right shape. Satisfied, he will cut a paper template and stick it on the stone so it can be cut out by someone else back in the workshop. This process uses a fretsaw with a carbon-iron wire, but the arch of the saw is traditional chestnut wood; it glistens with old age and use over the years. And so, piece by piece, Marco begins to build his blossoming rose, using a beeswax resin to glue the stone to its slate backing.

Depending on the size of the finished work, it may take hundreds, even thousands, of tiny pieces to complete—a fragment here, a sliver there, a crescent up here, each carefully selected to create the final, seamless picture without a hint that it is a mosaic of so many pieces. And the end result is, indeed, a picture. No, a photograph. Such is the perfection that it might well have been an instant caught by the camera's eye. They are objects of rare beauty that take months, years to produce.

'In six months, if he is clever, the artist can do something,' said Remo.

'That took the artist nine years,' he added, pointing to an exquisitely patterned tabletop hanging on a wall at the rear.

'What price? I've never put one on it. How do you price it?'

But then, with a merchant's pragmatism and an Italian's smile: 'Of course, there is always a price for something . . .'

And once you learn about the skill, artistry, time and value of the materials it is hard to disagree with him. They are not cheap, but then, to make them so would degrade them. Remo's particular pride is the creation of portraits, the way in which the artist must get the gradation of skin tone, the look in the eye, the play of light on the hair.

'Not everyone can do the face,' he said simply.

The inspiration for a mosaic work is as varied as the stones the artist will use to create it: the intricate swirls of the tabletop, for example; a still life; a young girl's bright smile; a landscape; a woman haggling with a stall owner over the cost of a fish on market day . . . Some are mischievous—art deco, and pop art that Andy Warhol might have imagined. The range of styles his six or eight artists employ is eclectic.

Sometimes it is the stone itself that provides the inspiration.

Remo showed us a Florence street scene. The artist, he said, had long wanted to reproduce it but could not find a stone with the right colour. Then kicking one day through the dirt in the hills above Florence, he found his stone and could proceed to produce his street scene. Many of the artists are also stone experts and locate many of their own stones in the field.

Interestingly, despite his admiration for the skill to produce a portrait and the patience to create a magnificent tabletop, Remo's own preferred piece is one that portrays imperfection. In his own modest way, Remo understood art as the maestro of marble, Michelangelo, did. *David* is notable not only for its grace and beauty but also for its blemishes—the disproportionately large head and hands.

Remo showed us a still life of a bunch of flowers, some in bud, some in full bloom and some withered and dead.

'The artist, he always wants to create the perfect picture. But this is real life. It is my favourite.'

Quarta Parte

Eat, drink and be Tuscan

Il vino é la poppo de' vecchi.
The wine is the breast (milk) of the elders.

Pane d'un giorno, vino d'un anno.
Bread is best a day old, wine a year old.

A tavola non s'invecchia.
At the table, one doesn't grow old.

—*Tuscan proverbs*

Eleven

Barring none

THOSE who have met me know that I am partial to a beer or four. In Italy, I have no fear of running dry.

Bars here are not just watering holes or places to meet friends. They are essential to the Italian way of life. They are places where you can get a drink, yes. But they can be— and most are—a one-stop community centre, convenience store, *gelateria* (ice-cream shop), snack food outlet, coffee shop, video parlour, telephone kiosk, card salon, pool hall, sweet shop, tearoom, postal centre, tobacconist and general hang-out place. If anything, drinking is the least important activity.

Bars here are like measles as a kid—you can't avoid them. They are also like the flies on the Chianina cattle in our fields each summer—ubiquitous. They are everywhere—the piazzas, side streets, alleyways, isolated country roads. The Piazza Garibaldi, in Sinalunga, has three fronting on to it. Our smaller Trequanda has the Bar La Siesta in its Piazza Garibaldi and the trendier Bar Paradiso of Giorgio on the outskirts. As in any country, some cater to different markets—youth, chic, trendy, wealthy, workers, daytime, night-time, singles, families. They can also be cheap or outrageously expensive.

Like most bar- or pub-goers, I like to have a 'regular' wherever I am. It's a bit like a favourite jersey, familiar and comfortable. You get to know the staff and the other regulars so you always feel welcome and have someone to chat with over a pint or whatever your tipple is. Here, Nancy and I have a network of favourites in the towns and cities we visit regularly. When I was in Boston, on a journey that I had no idea would lead me to Tuscany, I went to Cheers—and of course, nobody knew my name. Here, not only does nobody know my name but most staff don't even know my language. Yet you quickly learn the bar-survival basics: *birra* (beer), *alla spina* (tap beer), *bottiglia* (bottle), *spremuta* (freshly-squeezed citrus juice), *tramezzino* (sandwich), *panino* (bread roll), *vino rosso* (red wine), and the range of coffees—*cappuccino, espresso, caffè latte, caffè macchiato* . . .

The Bar La Siesta in Trequanda is, in many ways, the social centre of the town. It is on the top end of the row of buildings that line one side of the Piazza Garibaldi. Next door was the Emporium of young Silvia and Fabio before it closed down.

Opposite the bar is the *farmacia*, the pharmacy. The chemist regularly shuts up shop each day and strides purposefully across the piazza to get a shot of thick, black caffeine that fuels all Italians over, it seems, the age of five. Perhaps they get so much of it from their mother's milk as babies that it's like the addiction babies get while still in the womb of their drug-taking mother.

The bar is owned by Antonetta, a matronly woman in, I guess, her fifties. She can have a rather stern countenance but her smile lights up her face. The bar, like most in Italy, is a smallish affair—about the size of a living room in an average house. But she still manages to fit an astonishing range of merchandise into its confines. If I was of a mind, I could buy a coffee, hot tea, a post-card, a birthday card, a sandwich, a sweet pastry, chewing gum, a box of chocolates, a bottle of wine, a toy, a roll of sweets, a carton of cigarettes or a yoghurt, a Lotto ticket or a football pools coupon. I could play a video game or try my luck on the gambling machine. I could watch TV or I could make a telephone call. Or I could get a beer, sit at one of the four small tables and watch the many worlds of Italy come through the door.

It is a varied parade. Young mothers with babies in prams have a cappuccino and a pastry. Smartly-suited businessmen from Rome recharge themselves with an espresso shot before continuing their drive. Men sit at the table reading the newspaper the bar provides, a daily custom in every Italian bar. Old men just sit. Young kids buy sweets or sit perched before the video game. In summer, when the white plastic tables and chairs go out into the piazza under the now unfurled awning, tourists will write postcards, study maps or consult their guidebooks. To the winter-only Italian language will be added German, Dutch, French, English (both accents: England and America). Occasionally, an Australian accent might rise above the murmur. Once I even detected a Kiwi accent.

It is just as well for Antonetta that she has all these extras available. She certainly wouldn't make money if she relied on alcohol sales. It is the same in all the bars we frequent.

As far as I can determine, there are three 'markets' or customer types.

The first is no market at all. These are the people, mostly older men, who come to sit and talk about whatever it is that old men talk about—it can't be much in quiet little Trequanda. To these could be added the teenagers who gather on Sundays and after school to play the video machine or watch football on TV; in Grand Prix season they follow the fortunes of Ferrari with much passion. These people buy nothing. It amazes me how the owners allow them to take up space and seats that paying customers truly deserve. In summer, at the weekly market in Sinalunga's Piazza Garibaldi, we regulars of the Bar L'Angolo switch our allegiance to the bar on the opposite side of the piazza to escape the sun; the other is shaded outside. There are a couple of bench seats lining the wall and half a dozen tables on the piazza's cobblestones. These quickly get occupied by the townsfolk or marketgoers. They never buy anything; just sit and watch the world go by or chat with their friends. It is frustrating when paying customers such as ourselves cannot find a table or seat.

The second market is those who come to buy—but never alcohol. They may have a sandwich or a pastry, always a coffee, perhaps some cigarettes; may even be tourists looking for a postcard to send to the folks back home: 'Italy wonderful, Trequanda so cute.'

The choice of food is limited, boring and the same anywhere you go. Sandwiches—*tonno* (tuna), mozzarella cheese, prosciutto and *pomodori* (tomatoes) or a combination. The *panini*, bread rolls, offer the same exciting choices. Some more sophisticated places may offer a slice of spinach and ricotta cheese pie or flat *focaccia* bread made with olive oil and rosemary. And there are the sweet pastries; this is the land of the sweet tooth.

The third market actually buys a drink—an aperitif, glass of wine, maybe beer (although generally Italians are not beer drinkers) or a shot of the firewater, *grappa*. But always only one. The concept of an evening or after-work session at the bar is an alien one here. One shot and on your way.

I must confess that I am usually a Category Two customer. I rarely linger, although for a period I enjoyed a beer while Nancy was at her Italian lessons with Joe the German. It has an atmosphere that lacks the life and colour and crowd that makes a bar a social place. In the hour I was there, a steady stream of people came through the door, but never stayed long. At times, when Antonetta needed to buy something at the Co-op, I would be left alone guarding the premises.

If we decide to have a drink, it is invariably in another town. We do have another option in Trequanda, the Bar Paradiso. This is part of a row of shops out of the old town, on the road to Montisi and our road to San Clemente. Next door is the immaculate *macelleria* of our butcher Enrico. Luca the vet has his surgery in the same row. There are apartments above and Giorgio, the owner of the bar, often spends the night at the apartment of his mother above the bar to save the late-night drive back to his own place in Sinalunga.

The women friends and cousins who visit us take one look at Giorgio and a single word flashes into their minds: hunk. He's in his late twenties, tall, shaven-headed, bronzed and has a body that testifies to a serious attitude about working out. He speaks excellent English, is 'into' American in a big way (the bar wall is lined with black and white framed photos of American film or music stars, American blues drift out of his sound system and he frequently disappears to America in the winter off-season), mixes his own ice-cream (he has hopes of getting a chance or investor to open a *gelateria* in America; there was a possible opportunity at Caesar's Palace in Las Vegas but it melted away) and has his own business. He is, in the women's minds, eligible. Or, even better, someone they think it would be neat to have park his designer sneakers under their beds.

He has a curious approach to running a business.

In the six-months off-season he is open only on Friday, Saturday and Sunday nights. When I first came to Trequanda he didn't open until 9 p.m. Last summer, though, he added a pizzeria to his bar-cum-*gelateria* so began opening at 3 p.m. His bar attracts the trendy young things of the town; most come only for an ice-cream or the crêpes his kitchen also makes. When the tourists are here, they like to join the young set. In the six-month summer season, they spill out of the limited bar space into the big car park outside. Reiner the German refuses to drink there. 'Why I pay more money to drink in a car park?' he asked us one day.

We don't drink there because his prices are outrageously expensive, particularly for this area—L7000 ($NZ7) for a small bottle of beer, for example. One evening before we decided to boycott the bar, we waited to meet friends for a drink. I had two vodka-and-tonics and Nancy had a liqueur while we waited. We asked for the bill when the friends arrived, to 'square away' everything before we all got drinks. The cost was L21,000

($NZ21). We all decided it would be cheaper to go to the Commie bar in Sinalunga.

I was introduced to the Commie bar within the first week of my arrival in Tuscany. It is the ground floor of a house in the *Pieve* or new part of Sinalunga where it has spread down onto the Valdichiana. I don't know if it is owned by the local branch of the Reconstituted Communist Party that has its headquarters above. Nor if it is owned by the *pasticceria* that it shares the ground floor with. Or if it owns the bakery. Or if it's all one business.

The bakery produces the most exquisite pastries, cakes and tarts. Photographs of tiered wedding cakes and other temptations hang on the wall, so it presumably provides a catering service.

The Communist affiliation attracts a largely working class clientele. At lunchtime workmen in overalls come to the bar for a sandwich and to read the paper. There is one particularly loud-mouthed regular who is so self-opinionated that he tends to shout. Everyone in the bar knows what he thinks about football, politics or whether the moon is made of green cheese (or perhaps he is just hard of hearing). Sandwich in hand, he struts around the bar, bellowing in a deep bass voice.

The toilet is not overly clean and, worse, it's a hole-in-the-floor job which means squatting. With my creaky knees, this is no easy matter, particularly as there is no bar to cling to for support.

The whole business of doing your business in Italy is, so to speak, a hit-or-miss affair. Public toilets are something of a rarity here. And mostly they are pretty disgusting.

So it falls upon the bars to become the main source of R & R, release and relief. Your chance of finding a halfway decent one is a bit better than the odds of finding a clean public toilet. Some are filthy, some don't work, some are clogged with loo paper, none have a seat. But there are excellent ones to be found—clean, well-maintained, properly functional; these are the ones you always store mentally for later caught-short use.

Toilets, for obvious reasons, are an important part of the day for everyone. Hopefully, all of Italy will eventually come to understand this.

The Commie bar is where the 'Friday follies' gather each week. After buying our produce at the fruit and vegetable market that sets up a stall in a nearby car park each Friday, we drive the short distance to the bar to meet friends.

The regulars are Laura and one or both of the Finns, Lassi and Paivi. Sometimes our neighbour Airdrie comes. Steve the anxious American is a more recent addition to the gang.

We catch up with each other's news: how the tourist bookings are shaping up for the season, how the writing's coming on, hasn't the weather been dreadful . . . that sort of stuff. We swap yarns from our respective past lives and countries, tell war stories from our various travels and generally just 'shoot the breeze'.

It's a harmless endeavour but a valuable one as it binds our friendship and offers social contact.

We have another weekly rendezvous, on Tuesdays when the full market fills the town's Piazza Garibaldi. After doing whatever shopping we need, we adjourn to the Bar L'Angolo on the perimeter of the market. In winter, we are forced indoors to sit at one of the three small tables the young barstaff have managed to squeeze into its limited space. In warmer weather, we sit out in the sun at the ubiquitous white plastic tables set up along the bar's frontage. Sometimes we have to wait for a table, but never for long. Most customers prefer to stand at the bar and those who do sit stay just long enough to eat a pastry and drink a coffee.

The bar has its own morning rush hour. Between 11 and 11.30 it becomes crowded as the need for another caffeine shot strikes everyone. The bar fills with milling shoppers, stall holders and other locals. By 11.30, the place has cleared out so much that the staff can sweep the floor without working around anyone.

Over time, we got to recognise the locals: some of the older men would join us at our table, apparently desperate for company and conversation even if it has to be with *stranieri* who don't speak the language.

A less frequent locale in Sinalunga is the gloriously named Super Pizza Bros. Here we went to play pool with Hannalore and Reiner about once a month on Fridays after Hannalore's and Nancy's *ginnastica*, work-out class, in the Trequanda school, or more often on Saturday nights. It's on the top floor of a long office block on the steep hill down from the old town to the newer part of town. It is also a place where we can pretend to be in our twenties again as this is the hang-out for the town's young folk, before they head out for the discos.

Because it attracts the young set, it has a liveliness and buzz that other bars lack and we enjoy the atmosphere even though we're old enough to be the clientele's parents. Pop music blares from speakers, rock shows feature on the wall-mounted TVs, the screeches and whizz-bang noise from the video games reverberate around the room and the laughter of young friends meeting and horsing around brightens the air. The kids are anxious to look cool and sport the latest hairstyles (spikes for the guys this season) and clothes (those ridiculous chunky-sole shoes for the girls).

They're always well dressed—you have to search a long time to find a badly dressed Italian of any age—and well cleansed, apart from the designer stubble that's all the rage for any Italian male old enough to grow it. They are terrifyingly well behaved.

The bar is owned by the thirtyish Giorgio (no relation), who also sports a designer stubble, and his wife Silvia. Giorgio and his brother also own the bar at the *stazione*, the railway station at the foot of the hill. He speaks excellent English and hires only young staff who also speak English, a comfort to deal with when ordering. Last summer he leased some extra space adjacent to the original area, knocked down a wall and set up a pizzeria. His is one of the few places we have found locally that makes a halfway decent pizza. Most places simply offer a slab of thin pastry with tomato paste and a few dribbles of mozzarella cheese, if any. He at least has herbs like oreganum available. Tuscany is not renowned for pizza-making—its food is more peasant-based. And it shows in the miserable affairs most places turn out. We once decided to share a pizza in some long-forgotten restaurant. The menu offered a selection of toppings and we made our choice. On arrival at our table, the pizza boasted two thin slices of prosciutto, three thin slices of canned *funghi* that together would not have made a single little button mushroom and two thin slices of artichoke, *carciofi*. Unless desperate, we have given up ordering pizza in Tuscany; Naples, we have been told, is the pizza heaven of Italy but we have yet to go there.

Many bars in Italy have some space allotted for one or two pool tables, usually in a back room. Some also have a back room where men—never women—gather to play cards.

Super Pizza Bros' two pool tables are at least untorn or untaped, even if the surfaces are not quite true. Given the state of most we have come across, this is a petty complaint. The cues are also straight, something bordering on the miraculous. When we first started playing Giorgio was trying to organise a tournament and I was cajoled into parting with the L10,000 entry fee. In jest, I put down my address as 'New Zealand'; Giorgio immediately had visions of calling it an international event. The contest never eventuated, thank heavens, so I didn't have to make a fool of myself against any sharp young dude.

Pienza, Cortona, Montalcino, Montepulciano . . . we discover favourite hang-outs in each of the hilltop towns around us. Remarkably it is rare to see a drunk Italian. I can only ascribe it to the open attitude the people have towards alcohol. In my New Zealand and Nancy's America, drinking ages created mental temples of sin, forbidden fruits, of bars and pubs. Once legally allowed beyond those alluring portals, you wanted all you could taste, now.

We also explore the bars of the cities, but there we are more wary—the prices can be exorbitant. When Nancy first came to Italy we would sit in the expanse of Il Campo at Siena. The privilege of watching the world go by at an outside table would cost us L12,000 ($NZ12) for a glass of beer. In Florence's Piazza della Signorina, the cost jumped to L15,000.

So we learned quickly to seek the outlying places, the alleyway bars, the backstreet ones, where the locals went. In Siena, we discovered the Bar Centrale, its name bold in neon blue against the dark grey cobbles and stone of the street and buildings looming over its narrow passageway. It is just two streets back from Il Campo and in the heart of the old university district. The English school is about a hundred metres down the curving street. So the patrons, at lunchtime when we invariably go, are young student types. There are framed Art Nouveau posters of 1920s sailing ships on the wall and modern music over the speaker system.

Here we can sit at the bar and order our own fillings for a half-*panino*—mushrooms, fontina or mozzarella cheese, *pomodori*, *carciofi*, olive, prosciutto or speck (the very salty cured pork). We normally have it *caldo*, hot, toasted under a grill, and then have a *salsa piccante*, spicy mayonnaise, with it.

In earlier days, I went with a friend on Thursday nights to the Irish pub further up the street than the one our Bar Centrale runs off. It was a bizarre experience—listening to an Italian band playing Irish music in an Italian bar in Siena, drinking pints of Guinness or English beer. Inexplicably, they did not know 'Danny Boy'.

We would like to sit in Il Campo more, or, when in Florence, the Piazza della Signorina. But they remain formidably expensive. This whole pricing arrangement in the bars is a curious one, particularly in the larger towns and cities. If you sit at one of the tables, you will pay more than just standing at the bar. The *spina*, draught, beer is more expensive than the bottled. The wine is ridiculously cheap. Shots of Scotch are as much as the barman/woman decides you deserve—the price is the same. And, as you become a 'regular', the price of your booze will drop—you're a local now, not a *turista*. So now in our favourite haunts, we enjoy the beer and wine just a little more because it it discounted for us 'locals'.

Drinking is as much a part of the day as eating or getting out of bed each morning. In Trequanda, and other towns, it was quite common for the bar to be serving beer, wine or one of the Italian aperitifs that taste like cough medicine, at 10 or 10.30 in the morning. Often it would be people from the shops or businesses nearby; they would literally lock up shop and head for the bar to get a shot. One day I walked into the Bar La Siesta in mid-morning to get cigarettes. Two uniformed *carabinieri* were at the bar. They finished the espressos and then one ordered a glass of water and his companion ordered a glass of sparkling white wine. This seemed unreal—not only were they the guardians of the law but on duty and in uniform. I still cannot imagine a cop in, say, New Zealand or the United States or Britain even contemplating such an action, let alone the consequences if he or she was discovered drinking on the job.

I related this tale one Friday at our weekly gatherings in our Commie Bar.

'And at breakfast, they [Italians generally] will sometimes, have wine with breakfast,' observed one of our group.

'Really?' I asked with obvious ignorance.

'Oh, yes,' added Laura, 'Rosalbo often has a glass with breakfast.'

Given that many Italians save their appetites for a late-morning sandwich with coffee or better, the 1 p.m. starter's gun for lunch, I suspect that the early morning *vino* may not so much be with breakfast but instead of.

In fact, the early-bird habit had been reinforced that same Friday morning when we went to the Sinalunga fix-it and hard-ware shop with the ridiculous expectation that our grass trimmer would be ready just a week after leaving it for repairs. The always friendly, short, stout owner enveloped me with beer fumes as he explained why it wasn't ready. This was just after 10 a.m.

But you rarely see a drunk Italian weaving through the cobbled streets or creating some unpleasant scene in a bar. As the wine and post-dinner grappa begin to take effect, voices become more voluble, laughter more intensive and arm gesticu-lations more animated, although the last seems an impossibility with the Italian proclivity for holding conversations with their hands and arms.

149

On the autostrada, just north of the ring road around Pisa, we stopped for a stretch, toilet break and drink. These Autogrill stops (and those of competing companies) appear at regular intervals on the toll motorway. They do a brisk trade from travellers. They also provide a classic insight into the Italian relationship to the road. A sign behind the bar insisted that spirits above 21 per cent alcohol content would not be served between 10 at night and 6 the next morning. In other words, you could drink as much of whatever you wanted outside those hours. And even in that eight-hour 'safety on the road' time zone, you could drink as much beer or wine as your fancy dictated.

The young people drink little, unlike the young people in countries like New Zealand that have strict drinking age laws. My theory is that this is because from early childhood the Italians (and Europeans generally) are exposed to alcohol naturally—in the home, in restaurants and in the bars where they can come and go freely. In, say, New Zealand, bars and pubs are like forbidden fruit, fortresses of growing temptation waiting to be assaulted when the magical birthday comes and they gain right of entry. Although they get hold of alcohol before that in that mysterious way that teenagers develop, they are not trained to handle drinking; it is an unnatural part of their lives rather than an accepted part of their day-to-day environment. So their attitude when unleashed by the law is to drink as much and as often as possible. It's an unhealthy system and countries where it is practised would do much to learn from the European model.

This take-it-or-leave-it attitude by the young in Italy is readily evident. They come to bars to socialise in groups. One or two may have a beer, another might have one of those ghastly aperitifs, as vile but with a sharper taste than the white and treacly cod-liver oil mixture my mother thrust down my throat to ward off a childhood cold (a useless torture, I have learned, as there is no cure for the cold), but the others will just hang out laughing and chatting as teenagers do.

Nancy once asked two young men—both eighteen—taking her English language class what the drinking age was. They didn't know if there even was one and if so, what it might be.

'It doesn't matter. It's always there,' one told her. One didn't drink at all; the other confessed to enjoying a beer occasionally but mostly he drank Coke.

Instead of the local bar, the teens head for the nearest disco. The countryside around here is littered with them. They are vast affairs, capable of holding thousands. One, Blu Kaos, is on the outskirts of Monte San Savino about twenty kilometres from San Clemente. Its three rooms can host 5000 energetic young Italians. The town, perhaps a little bigger than Trequanda, boasts not just Blu Kaos but another disco as well and together they probably support a Saturday night population four or five times the town's. Another is opposite the nearest exit from the autostrada at Bettolle, again on the outskirts. Nancy once went there at the regular end-of-the-season outing of her *ginnastica* class. Of the twenty or so women who went, no one bought a drink that night.

It's not hard to understand why the disco-goers don't bother drinking in these establishments. The entrance price is L25,000 ($NZ25) and a small beer costs L10,000 ($NZ10). You pay heavily for your saturday night fever in Italy.

Twelve

Making a meal of it

THE Tuscan dining experience is not so much a necessity of life as life itself. It is like a religious experience and is approached with an appropriate sense of respect, if not awe. The seriousness with which Italians view their food was vividly described to Nancy by Joe, her Italian teacher in Petroio, the nearby village that has proclaimed itself the 'Terracotta Capital of the World'. Fortified by this appellation, the town dignitaries decided to hold an annual terracotta festival and a meeting was arranged to discuss the form and content. Perhaps because he was a *straniero* who would open the mysterious doors into the outside world, Joe was invited to participate and only turned up at the first committee meeting prepared to offer ideas. 'The meeting was supposed to start at 9 p.m.,' Joe reported later. 'But it didn't get going until 9.45 p.m. because the Mayor didn't arrive until then.' Joe remained until a little after midnight—and even then the discussion was still firmly focused on what food stalls should be in the streets during the week of the festival. Joe said he kept trying to bring up ideas for the music. 'They would say, "yes, interesting", but then get back to the food.' He walked out in disgust, while the debate about the food continued to rage.

On another occasion he encountered the same passion for food that is on display at every fair, fête and festival. This was the annual donkey race at Torrita di Siena. These festivals usually last a week, culminating in the big event, whatever it might be. The festival committee had organised a progressive dinner among the local restaurants—antipasto here, pasta there, meat course down that road, and so on. The price was reasonable so Joe and his wife bought a ticket and duly turned up on the appointed day—along with half the population of the Valdichiana. Knowing the Italian penchant for eating, they had turned up earlier than the official start time. But so had everyone else.

They queued for half an hour to get their *antipasti*. They queued for half an hour for their pasta before giving up and moving on to the stall with the meat course—another half hour. They found a table before realising they had to go to yet another stall and stand in line for wine. Then they returned to the pasta line; it was even longer than before. In disgust, they went home, defeated by the locals' insatiable appetites.

Mealtime is also an important social occasion, a time for extended families to gather or friends to exchange gossip. Restaurant tables are constantly rearranged as parties of diners come and go.

In a country with such high unemployment and low wages, it is astonishing how often people eat out. Lunch, *pranzo*, is equally important as dinner, *cena*. Both require several hours to cope with the endless food, the flowing wine, the post-meal relaxation for digestion, and to allow all the news to be canvassed properly.

There is certainly no lack of opportunity to enjoy the Italian dining experience. *Trattorie*, *ristoranti*, *osterie* are as ubiquitous as the sunflowers of summer. Many, like the sunflowers, are out in the Tuscan countryside, standing in splendid isolation in locations that seem so far off the beaten track that it is impossible for them to be economically viable. But the Italian nose sniffs them out and they always have diners. Some make their continuing existence even more of an economic miracle by closing most or all of the week in the undoubtedly leaner times between tourist seasons.

I am accustomed to calling a restaurant just that, a restaurant. But here there are demarcation lines that define a particular establishment. A trattoria, for example, is a small restaurant, according to our well-used Webster's New World Italian dictionary. A *ristorante*, it tells us, is exactly that, a restaurant. A *ristorante della stazione* has a less glamorous definition—station buffet. An *osteria* is simply an 'inn'. These distinctions mean little to us in our poverty-line days at San Clemente. We look for more easily distinguishable signs of dining-out suitability—the price list on the menus at the entrance to every restaurant. And we also learn to avoid restaurants with pre-mealtime tables already set out with cloth napkins, silverware and other sure signals of expensive dining.

Still, our parsimony has not stopped us from enjoying—no, living—the Italian dining experience from time to time. It is as unavoidable and ubiquitous as the wild poppies of spring. There are restaurants around us that offer excellent fare—most of it utilising the glorious produce of the hills and fields and prepared as typically Tuscan dishes.

There are three styles of menu and service we discovered in our travel through the world of Tuscan dining. Some, like the one I take my tour parties to at the spa village of Bagno Vignoni, is of the service counter variety. The restaurant is at the entranceway to the village proper. We drive up the hill off the main road, immediately past the bridge over the River Orcia. The town spreads back from the cliff carved over the centuries by the river below. At the top of the hill there is a large car park that in summer swells with tour buses, camper vans, and cars bearing the number plates of a continent—GB (Britain), D (Deutschland, Germany), F (France), CH (Switzerland), even I (Italy). This is—and has been over many centuries—a popular tourist spa with its spring-fed, thermally heated mineral waters.

We walk up the road towards the small village, past the wrought-iron fence separating the street from the tree-studded park. At the end of the park is a small square. The restaurant is at the rear—a tiny doorway and two or three steps down into the interior. To the right are a meagre offering of small tables with two or three chairs each, more of a token gesture really because when the 'season' is in full swing most people eat outside at large bench-seating picnic tables set under a canopy of trees. The warmth of the air and the cool of the shade provide a pleasant combination and ambience to enjoy the food we have selected from behind the glass counter that greets us as we enter.

In time, as my weekly tour visits continue, the young women behind the counter recognise me and always extend a warm smile of welcome. Also, the price I pay seems to drop. This is not uncommon in Italy—there is one price for tourists, top price, on the basis that they won't be coming back so get their money before someone else does; they can afford it, anyway, they're tourists, aren't they? Then there is the price that locals pay, a considerable discount on the top whack the hapless tourist has to fork out. This 'local' price is presumably on the basis that a) they're Italian and b) they're regulars so we'll get their money eventually. You can go to the same restaurant and order the same menu items and you will pay a different price each time.

I seem to fall into some economic crack between the two: I'm obviously a *straniero* but I'm also a regular. And I'm bringing extra money through the door with my little tour groups. Behind the glass front of the counter is the house selection. From the row of plastic containers I select servings of artichokes, *carciofi*, steeped in extra-virgin olive oil; slices of roasted *melanzana*, eggplant, also in a bath of oil; strips of roasted red *peperoni*, peppers, rolled and stuffed with a spicy minced vegetable mix that appears to be based around *carote*, carrots; small, flat cocktail-type *cipollini*, onions, soaked in an unknown liquid that gives them a sweet-and-tart flavour; button mushrooms, *funghi*, again dressed with oil and, perhaps, some herbs.

All these are heaped on to paper plates—this is very much a throw-away establishment. It is tiny and has no room to provide a kitchen in which to cook an *à la carte* menu, let alone space for a dish-washing area to cater for the volume of the crockery and cutlery that its high-season luncheon crowd of seventy or eighty would produce. So, to go with our paper plates, we are also handed paper place mats, plastic knives and forks in a sealed plastic bag like the ones you get on airlines, and plastic glasses for the water we also order. The only concession made to 'normal' dining is the glasses for our bottle of *vino locale*, one of the locally-produced wines they stock.

While this selection is being made, one of the women is out in the kitchen preparing our *bruschette con pomodori, olio e aglio*, toasted slices of bread with raw tomatoes, olive oil and garlic.

Then I choose from the variety of salamis and *prosciutti*, cured hams, on the next level down behind the glass front of the counter. Normally, I ask for slices of the *salume cinghiale*, wild boar salami that is very much a Tuscan speciality, as is game food generally. To this is added slices of pecorino cheese. Most local cheese, like pecorino, is made from ewe's milk rather than cow's. It comes in three forms: fresco (fresh), *semi stagionato* (partly-matured) and *stagionato* (fully-matured). I normally order the last for its stronger flavour.

While all this is going on my band of tourists have been reformed into a delivery service, coming to and fro to collect our paraphernalia for lunch *al fresco*—table mats, plates, cutlery, a plate of sliced bread, glasses, bottles of wine and water, plates of vegetables, cold meats and cheese and, finally, the *bruschette* as they begin to emerge from the kitchen. Leaving them to set up the outside table, I pay the bill, which has, apart from the wine, water and *bruschette*, been calculated by weight.

And so we sit at our picnic table under the trees, passing the plates among ourselves, selecting this, choosing that, rejecting those, sipping our wine and water, tearing our bread into bite-sized chunks and watching the world go by. It is a rather bucolic experience and one that my tourists always enjoy—the food, the ambience, the conversation ... Later, we will dispose of our throw-away implements in the rubbish bins provided and stroll back down the street, past the car park, to the stream carrying the overflow from the springs in the town's piazza. There we plunge our feet into the sensuous warmth of the mineral-laden water, sitting on the bank and just relaxing in a post-luncheon idyll before moving on to a mini-tour of Pienza.

This self-service, little-bit-of-this, little-bit-of-that style of dining is fine for what I imagine the natives regard as namby-pamby tourists, but no self-respecting Italian would sit down to *pranzo*, let alone *cena*, with such a miserably skimpy luncheon ration. If you are going to eat an Italian lunch, you must think Italian. The size of the Italian lunch isn't so important. What is important is that it is a cooked lunch that includes pasta and bread, usually with a bit of salad and wine.

This is the full sit-down, stay-for-hours, slap-up meal at the *trattoria*, *ristorante* or *osteria* of your choice. It is like embarking on a culinary crusade against the heretics of fast food and bar snacks. It is being Italian.

There are two formulae for paying, but only one, undeviating, rigid formula for dining. The less common of the paying formulae is the *prezzo fisso*, fixed price. But it is generally the safer, price-wise at least. The second is the traditional *à la carte* system, paying by dish and drinks.

The *prezzo fisso* menu includes all your drinks as well as mountains of food. Pre-dinner drink, *signore? Non problema*. The wine is delivered as a matter of course. Perhaps a *limoncello* to follow? And a *grappa* to finish? The bottles are usually left on the table to help yourself.

First, though, a guided tour of the Italian meal.

A meal out at a Tuscan restaurant follows a fixed routine. The system is as inflexible as the hard gaze of an Italian starer. The decoration may be different, the layout too. The food may be prepared differently, the ambience may differ by shades. But the courses, the menu, will adhere to a ritual that you suspect has been passed down over the centuries from generation to generation like a family heirloom. Italy is a conservative nation, rural Tuscany even more so.

First, baskets or plates of sliced bread are offered while you review the menu, order your preference and wait for the first course. Even if you do not want bread, preferring to wait for the meal proper, it will be delivered: it serves as a sort of cover charge, maybe to cover the cost of dishwashing and laundering. Wine and water arrive, too. In the cheaper establishments we frequent, we simply order *vino da tavola*, a carafe of the house wine, cheap and cheerful and probably purchased in bulk from the local wine co-operative. Bottles of water, *naturale* (still) or *frizzante* (gassy) are also *de rigueur*. The bigger glass, protocol insists, is for the water; the smaller for the wine.

And thus to the first course, the *antipasto*. This can vary from restaurant to restaurant, but usually only within a limited range; slices of *prosciutto crudo* (cured ham) or salamis (Tuscan favourites—fennel-flavoured or wild boar); *crostini* with a savoury spread or *bruschette*.

In Italy this is not, in fact, the first course, merely the appetite-whetter. The *primi*, the true first course, is the stomach-buster. Great mountains of pasta or risotto or gnocchi (potato balls in a sauce) or thick soups swollen by bread or beans. This is the fill-'er-up course and with my bird-peck appetite I learnt to avoid it if paying course by course.

The *secondo*, second course is some sort of meat dish, normally roasted or grilled. Vegetables or salad are an optional extra in *à la carte* restaurants but always provided in the *prezzo fisso* establishments. Finally, a tooth-rotting dolce selection; Italians have enormously sweet teeth and attack the flans and *gelati*, ice-creams and cakes with gusto.

These affairs are not eat-it-and-run occasions. They are to be savoured, to be lingered over, as a renewal of life. They are wonderful.

Our local Trequanda *ristorante*, Conte Matto, was put to good use on occasion, particularly when we had visitors. It was just behind the Piazza Garibaldi, and in summer would spill out into a small section off the piazza with a raised wooden deck of a few tables.

It was both a fixed-price and *à la carte* establishment and our friend from Miciano, the holiday apartment block created from an old abbey further down our dirt lane, was sure it, too, was in the Michelin guide, although we never confirmed this.

Bronek and his wife Vera came late into our Tuscan life. He had been working for the United Nations, in charge of food aid distribution for south Asia, based in Pakistan. He was originally from a part of Poland that is now Russian. He grew up in England, he lived in Italy for a time and he travelled widely in his career. He spoke five or six languages fluently. I once asked him what he regarded himself as. 'I feel like a European.' Before joining the UN he had worked for the Greek shipping tycoon Onassis at his Monte Carlo offices. They had an apartment right on the waterfront, overlooking the start-finish line of the Monte Carlo Grand Prix.

When we met them, Bronek had just retired. But the organisation kept hauling him back for active duty—to handle the investigation of a UN plane crash, then a five-month stint in charge of aid distribution in Ethiopia. They made a special detour to Miciano in our final week just to say goodbye.

But back to Conte Matto. The woman who owns it deserves some sort of medal. She and her husband moved to Trequanda to run the restaurant some years before I arrived. But within a few weeks her husband died suddenly, leaving her with not only a new business representing their savings, but two young children. She stuck with it and it is now a thriving little concern. It has an impressive *antipasti* line-up on a table in the middle of the dining room—*crostini*, onion, eggplant, peppers, salamis, hard-boiled eggs, about twenty selections you could pick yourself or get the waiting staff—Madam's now grown-up children—to choose for you.

There was a respectable *primi* (pasta) selection and an excellent *secondi* menu. By now, I had learnt to avoid the pasta and opted just for the *secondo*. Invariably, I chose the wild boar ragout—a hearty, herb-scented stew rich with gamey flavour. Nancy's favourite was the roasted duck, again crusted with herbs.

Each year, during the month-long *Estate Trequanda*, Summer in Trequanda, festival, Il Conte Matto would put on an open-air meal in the piazza itself. This was always an anticipated affair and attracted perhaps two hundred locals and holidaymakers alike to the long trestle tables under the stars, awaiting the procession of food and the bottles of *vino*.

A regular haunt (if regular can be used to describe our infrequent indulgences) is the Osteria delle Grotte, at the top of the steep hill that leads up from the *stazione* to the old town in Sinalunga. The name is apt as its long narrow dining room has been carved, cave-like, into the rock just below the old town wall. But there is also an outside terrazzo where it is a total joy to sit on a summer's evening in the warm air, under trees whose leaves brighten in soft lighting.

'Le Grotte', as it in known by everyone, is a *prezzo fisso*, and owned by Luigi, a stout man in, perhaps, his late fifties. His smile of welcome and table visits are as warm as the air that floats serenely around us. In winter, the terrazzo is shut down and we all sit inside warmed now by a gently flaming artificial open fire. As the room is narrow, there is only enough room for a row of tables down each side with a serving aisle separating the diners. The bar is at one end of the room, the kitchens at the other.

Prezzo fisso can also be translated as 'fixed menu'. We have no choice in the matter; what the restaurant ordains, we will eat that day. This is fine in itself, since it removes any uncertainties that you may be unwittingly ordering turnips or, worse, tripe. Or some other such culinary disaster like the nasty bits and pieces of assorted animals we encounter at Enrico's, our butcher in Trequanda: one day I came back to San Clemente breathlessly swearing that there were pigs' penises available. Nancy and our guests were so impressed that we all duly marched into his shop the next day. They refused to believe it, although there was a remarkable resemblance, even if we had never really examined a pig's penis closely before this. In the end, we decided it was pig's tail that had somehow lost its curl. Still, what on earth would you have to do to a pig's tail to make it edible? It remains one of the unsolved mysteries of Italian culture.

But there are risks. You *may* actually be served turnips or tripe or some part of a pig's anatomy that you never imagined could be turned into anything edible, let alone tasty. Fortunately, that has never happened at Luigi's Le Grotte and the food has always been excellent, if too lavish. Fortunately, too, our first visit was with Laura and Rosalbo. The latter is a long-time friend of Luigi so, even better, was able to negotiate a special rate. With Rosalbo as our tutor we were not confused by the lack of a menu; the concept of the price-fixed menu was explained to us ignorant *stranieri* used to ordering our filet mignons with or without the mushrooms, our mussel starter rather than the mustard kidneys.

It was only on later outings that we discovered another dining danger. While the *antipasti* and *primi* courses always differed, the *secondo* never changed. It was always quarters of duck and a baked roll of stuffed minced rabbit. Always. Not only did we not particularly care for the rabbit (the duck was always delicious) but the repetitiveness of it dulled our enjoyment of what was otherwise an excellent night out. Still summer evenings on the terrace with vines threaded through the overhead beams were as memorable as winter evenings in the closed-off restaurant proper with its blazing gas-fed fire.

But a very real fire warmed the big dining room at the unadvertised farm restaurant we discovered thanks to Hannalore and Reiner. It was off the road to Pienza, just a dirt lane turn-off that you'd miss if you were blinking. You drove about a kilometre on the pot-holed lane, winding past fields and woods, before a final turn up a steep little drive into the open area for parking. It was very much a working farm—ploughs, tractors and other agricultural impediments vied for space with the cars of those diners who had already arrived.

I can't recall the name of the establishment or if, in fact, it even had one. It apparently opened for business only one

Saturday night a month and a table on those nights was keenly sought, particularly by the residents of Pienza who used it as a quiet refuge from the constant flow of tourists in their town and its few restaurants—even in mid-winter when we went.

Obviously the secret was spreading as a large room had been added on to the farmhouse. This was the dining room. It connected on the back wall to the farm's kitchen and from here a constant stream of the farm family emerged with plates and wine.

The food wasn't particularly memorable; it was the atmosphere of the room that gave the night the flavour of an Italian meal. It was really just a pizzeria with some side salads served, not a proper restaurant. The owner was Swiss and the only memorable thing I ate was the homemade bread, which definitely wasn't Italian—it had flavour.

The large room was filled with long wooden tables capable of seating a dozen or so diners—and most were filled with parties that large. But it was dominated by the big open fireplace. Huge logs, burning quietly rather than roaring, threw a constant sheet of heat into the room—an invisible horizontal cascade.

Already, young children were sitting on the wide, raised hearth or running around between tables. When an Italian family goes out to eat, the whole family goes—babies, toddlers, young-sters, teenagers, mama and papa and, if they are still alive and local, grandfather and grandmother. In stuffy New Zealand, the presence of young children in a restaurant is rather frowned upon. The attitude is: this is grown-ups' territory and time, leave the kids at home. To Italians, this would be unthinkable. Eating is life and, anyway, the kids need to learn about socialising and restaurant customs as early as possible because they'll be doing plenty of it over the next sixty or seventy years. It's a healthy attitude and everyone easily accepts their ever-moving presence. They are not an intrusion. They are not an annoyance. They are simply . . . there. In fact they provide great entertainment with their laughter and running around.

In a small rural community, most people get to know each other, which was obviously the case this night. As the food continued and the *vino* flowed, people began migrating between tables to chat with friends or, maybe, neighbours. Others, including myself, sat on the hearth for a time; I even managed to get into a conversation with people from other tables.

The atmosphere throughout was relaxed, happy, a celebration of family and friends, a renewed affirmation of life as it should be. How sad that stiff and formal societies like New Zealand can't embrace this attitude. It brings spirit and sheer enjoyment to an evening out in a restaurant.

There were two restaurants close to San Clemente where, however, such exuberance would be frowned upon. Within a fifteen-minute drive are two of Tuscany's—some say Italy's—most highly-regarded establishments, both Michelin-rated.

La Chiusa was on a side road also off the road to Pienza. We had never seen it. But l'Amorosa had been a familiar sight as it sat at the corner where the road down the hill from Petroio to the Valdichiana valley floor meets the road between Sinalunga and Torrita di Siena. We passed it regularly, a large walled complex on a slight rise above the road down from San Clemente. In front of it was its line of tall at-attention cypresses flanking the narrow dirt lane leading up to it, about forty on each side.

Over our years at San Clemente, we had heard glowing reports of the food at each restaurant and alarming ones of the fearsome cost of sampling it. We were like two kids in front of the sweet shop window and with no pocket money left; we could look, we could dream, but the goodies on show might well have been on the moon. But as I knew I wanted to write about the Italian dining experience, it seemed important to visit one even if just to talk about how a Michelin-starred restaurant takes itself above the typical Tuscan cuisine.

Nancy had already been to l'Amorosa, for a *caffè* with Emma and Luigi and one of their friends (cost for three espressos and a *caffè macchiato*, espresso with steamed milk, 17,000 lire, so we had confirmation of the pricing regime) and reported on its beautiful setting.

So l'Amorosa it was to be. I decided on a cunning plan—go

late morning, mid-week when it was least likely to be busy and guests staying in the hotel part of the operation would be out sightseeing. Not only would the owner and staff be more readily accessible but maybe, at slow period, we might be asked to sample the luncheon menu.

Cheeky? Certainly. But over many years as a journalist, you learn to be cheeky, imaginative and bold to get the information you need.

Nancy's reporting was accurate as we drove up that cypress-lined road to the walls of the old fortified village one Wednesday morning. The firs, drawing together in the distance, are like the walls of a funnel, drawing you through them with no chance of escape. But escape was the last thing on our minds.

L'Amorosa can trace its roots back to the 1300s, when it was built as a fortified village to protect against the many human predators that passed below it—the Valdichiana has always been a vital strategic thoroughfare between Rome and the north. Hannibal marched through, as did his archenemies, the Caesars and their armies. Invaders from the north used its flatness as a perfect direct route for their assaults on Rome. Hitler's armies marched by—and fled back as the Allies advanced from Rome.

Just fifteen years after the Great Plague of 1348 decimated Siena, killing three out of every four citizens, the important Battle of the Valdichiana raged around it. A Florence-paid mercenary company from Brittany met a Sienese army in battle on the ground between Sinalunga and Torrita di Siena in October 1363. The cocky Bretons, led by a Niccolo da Montefeltro, were soundly thrashed and the leader taken prisoner, along with many of his troops.

Painter Lippo Vanni's depiction—celebration—of the victory clearly includes l'Amorosa. The great fresco is now in the Sala del Mappamondo in Siena's Palazzo Pubblico.

Today, the fortifications—the walls, the tower—provide shelter of a more peaceful pursuit. As you walk through the thick arched doorway, a deep and wide open piazza greets you. This is the focus of the whole Amorosa complex. Here, over the centuries, the villagers farming the land would gather for festivals and important meetings. The piazza, perhaps fifty or sixty metres deep and twenty wide, is surrounded by two-storey brick buildings. On the immediate left is a wide stairway leading up to the old lord's villa. Today, the current owner Carlo Citterio lives there. At the far end is the rather stark façade of the little church that has provided comfort and, presumably, faith for the generations of villagers who have lived in and around the walls. On its left are the *osteria* and wine bar, made from the old cellars of the farm. On the right side of the piazza is a glorious two-storied sweep of brick-arched verandas and walkways, cascades of pink geraniums flowing down from the low top-storey walls between the arches. The hotel suites begin at the far end and then move around the back, away from the piazza. On the immediate right is the restaurant, built in the former stables. A high clock tower divides the hotel suites and the hotel reception/lobby and restaurant. If the piazza is the dominant feature of the complex, the well in its centre is its focus—a brick structure with its rounded base and high, arched, drawing-bucket support structure.

Behind this central area are gardens and lawns. On a lower terrace at the back is an enormous herb garden that supplies the restaurant's needs. It even has exotic plants not readily available in the local area—horseradish and ginger, for example. Elsewhere, a large swimming pool with beautiful views of the countryside is available, one end unwalled so it provides a waterfall lip effect.

But we are here to find out about fine Tuscan cuisine and how, or even if, it differs from the fare in an everyday *ristorante*. Our first appointment is with Walter Redaelli, the chef. He originates from Como, in the north, and had been a chef for some fourteen years when we met him. He trained at a chalet school in Paris and had worked in France and Milan.

He describes the cuisine of Tuscany as 'more complete' than say, the fish-based food of the Mediterranean or the country cooking of the French interior.

'Here you can have the food of the sea, the country and the mountains [of Tuscany]'.

His kitchen, he says, is very seasonal. It has to be, as nothing is frozen; all the food is fresh. He himself selects the vegetables and fruits from the market in nearby Torrita di Siena that is open three or four days a week. The cheese also comes from nearby Torrita, the salamis from Belsedere, a working farm/holiday apartment complex just outside Trequanda.

His only real problem is getting good quality tropical fruit. 'There is no big city near so it is difficult to find.'

The cellar holds 7000 bottles of wine. 'But it is never enough as the restaurant is always fully booked.' The majority (eighty per cent) of the wines are Tuscan and the rest from other parts of Italy like Piedmont in the north or from the deep south. It is all Italian wine. The most expensive is a 1990 Brunello *Riserva* from nearby Montalcino. A bottle to wash down your meal will cost you L260,000. The restaurant makes its own *gelato* (ice-cream), pasta and pastries, including his favourite on the menu, the *focaccia di mandorle*, almond shortbread, that has been a feature of the restaurant for twenty-five years. As befits a seasonal restaurant, dependent on the fresh fruit and vegetables available at any given time, the menu is a moving feast, changing every two or so months.

The owner, Carlo Citterio, is a tall white-haired gentleman dressed, surprisingly, in shabby old workman's clothes. The reason became clear when I asked for a photograph. He refused, insisting that the staff (impeccably uniformed), the atmosphere and the restaurant were the important elements of l'Amorosa, not him. He was a behind-the-scenes, 'hands-off-the-clients-but-hands-on-the-hard work' owner. That morning, the crisis-of-the-day he was attending to involved the water from the well.

L'Amorosa was a wedding present from his mother, whose family had owned the property since 1873. Apart from the old village complex, there are some three hundred hectares of land surrounding it. These had been divided between himself and his sister.

His piece includes twenty hectares of vineyards, producing 900,000 litres of wine a year, the bulk sold to other producers.

'The olive trees? They're only for looks. We're not on top of a hill so this area is no good for olives.'

The hotel has twenty rooms with plenty of space for expansion in the old granaries and farm buildings behind the piazza that had not yet been restored.

'But if we did expand, it would be no bigger than thirty rooms total. I want to keep it tranquil and each client needs a corner [of the property] for himself.'

The restaurant was opened in 1971; the hotel began in the 1980s. He never has to advertise either. Seventy-five per cent of the guests are *stranieri*; of those, seventy-five per cent are American. That's not surprising as they are probably the best able to afford a room for the night. A standard double room costs L390,000 and a top-of-the-line suite L590,000. If you really want space and privacy, the sole apartment *Le Vigne*, The Vineyards, comes at L1,200,000 a night.

My cunning plan worked as he invited us to have lunch. We weren't about to refuse.

Its long, narrowish room can seat about fifty people. The walls are bare brick, as are the vaulted ceilings and archways that break up the space with understated subtlety.

Alessandro, the *maître d'* or restaurant manager, suggested we leave it to him to bring a selection of dishes that reflected the menu and the food. We were happy to agree.

Our table had none of the usual trimmings like oil, vinegar, salt and pepper. The warning was implicit: Here we cook to perfection, you will not need—or want—to spoil what we offer with your own clumsy tastes and, in fact, we didn't need them. Neither was there a line-up of wine glasses. As each course was served, a glass of wine that perfectly complemented it was poured from an already-opened bottle; it, like all the cutlery, was changed with each serving.

So here's how to dine Michelin-style in Tuscany.

1. Baby roasted zucchini, sliced, and served with a subtle freshly made balsamic vinegar, basil and honey sauce.

2. Chilled mosaic of zucchini and eggplant slices pressed around romano cheese and cherry tomatoes with basil and with a drizzle of special balsamic vinegar from Reggio Emilio—'You can drink it like a sweet wine,' said Alessandro, offering a teaspoonful separately. He was right; it had a glorious, sweet taste with no vinegary harshness whatsoever.

3. 'Stracci' pasta with fresh herbs. There were ten separate herbs but you couldn't pick them out individually because they all melded together so completely.

4. A wonderful sorbet with sage and lemon; not a hint of sweetness, just an exquisite taste to clear the palate.

5. Pork fillet with prunes and pears, zucchini and potato shoe-strings and a roasted tomato also topped with prunes and pears.

We later worked out that the cost, if we had been paying, would have been around L120,000 each, without the wine.

We could, for L100,000 each, (excluding wine) have had the fixed-price luncheon menu; guinea-hen mosaic with shrimps in grape sauce; eggplant timbale with herb and tomato sauce; gilthead in paper casing flavoured with Vernaccia (white wine) from San Gimignano; the sage sorbet; sirloin steak of Chianina veal in a herb and porcini mushroom crust; wild berries in a basket with ice-cream and raspberry sauce; 'coffee and frivolities'.

Or we could have just ordered from the *à la carte* menu. Some selections: octopus salad with potatoes and olives (L25,000); cannelloni white bean salad with chives, shrimp, celery and grey mullet caviar (L26,000); cream of potato and lobster soup (L25,000); a 'curl' of eel from Lake Trasimeno with celery purée (L37,000); *bistecca Fiorentina* T-bone steak, two people minimum (L95,000); saddle and livers of rabbit with rosemary (L37,000).

Before we left—or, rather, waddled away from—l'Amorosa and its restaurant, I timorously asked Walter if he might share some of his recipes. Unlike most chefs, who guard their recipes like the Queen does her Crown Jewels, this was no problem. I am usually reluctant to include recipes in a book, but here is a sampling of Chef Walter Redaelli's favourites from the recipe pages of l'Amorosa. It is something you can try safely at home.

PASTA

Homemade '*stracci*' pasta with a mixed fresh herb sauce. Ingredients for four people.

fresh pasta	100 g
fresh tomato	100 g
parsley	10 g
basil, marjoram	5 g (each)
thyme, sage, rosemary, nipitella (Italian herb, optional), mint, lemon balm, tarragon	2 g (each)
sheep cheese	5 g
salt and pepper	50 g
extra-virgin olive oil	200 g

Procedure

Cut pasta into 6 cm pieces. Clean the fresh herbs in water and dry well with a clean, dry cloth. Finally, chop the herbs and place in a mixing bowl with the olive oil and salt and pepper. Mix well.

Cook the pasta in boiling salted water for three minutes, drain and add to the oil and herbs previously prepared. Add the grated sheep cheese and serve with a dusting of fresh tomato, previously cut into thin slices.

MAIN

Rabbit with fennel flowers (*coniglio ai fiori di finocchi*). Ingredients for four people.

one rabbit, jointed	
white wine	120 mls
butter	150 g
fennel flowers	4 g
fondo bruno (brown stock)	200 mls
salt and pepper to taste	

Procedure

Lightly brown the rabbit in a casserole dish with the butter over a low flame. It should have been previously salted, peppered and sprinkled with the fennel flowers. Leave to cook in the oven at 160°C for twenty-five minutes.

In the last few minutes of cooking, take out the rabbit and skim off the fat that has formed, taking care not to throw away any of the fennel flowers. Wet the used casserole with the white wine, leave to evaporate over a flame and add the brown stock. Boil for a few minutes.

Debone the rabbit, cut the meat into pieces and place on a plate. Cover with the sauce.

DESSERT

Almond shortbread (*focaccia di mandorle*). Ingredients for four people.

blanched almonds	150 g
sugar	150 g
flour	150 g
butter	150 g

Procedure

Mince the almonds and butter. Add to the flour and sugar to obtain a firm dough. Roll out into two thin discs and cook at 160°C for ten minutes.

Unite the discs with a thin layer of baker's custard between them. Lightly dust with icing sugar.

An alternative ancient Tuscan recipe you might not want to try at home is 'pluck of lamb': cut up the lamb's pluck—liver, lungs, heart and spleen—into walnut-sized pieces; add a sprig of rosemary and chopped onion; cover it well with olive oil, salt and pepper; add a half cup of white wine; reduce the sauce then add fresh, ripe tomatoes and a little broth; cook for 20 minutes until the liquid has evaporated leaving a thick stew 'which would bring back the dead'—or help you join them.

As Walter and Alessandro invite in the menu, '*Buon appetito*'.

It's a refrain that rings around every city, town, village, hamlet and home every day in Tuscany.

Quinta Parte

Il Palio di Siena

This (the Palio) is a festival with
profound roots in the local culture.
It is central to our identity.

—Roberto Barzanti, former Mayor of Siena

This is war, this is not a
pretty horse race.

—Palio aficionado

Thirteen

The Palio and the ghettos of passion

$\mathcal{A}$T seventy-five seconds, it lasts somewhat longer than the first sexual encounter of a teenage boy. It has all the emotion, excitement, tension, passion, lust and, yes, terror that accompanies his experience. But for the people of Siena, Il Palio is more than a transitory sexual high. It is a transcendental ritual, a call to arms, a rite of passage, a way of life and a celebration of being Sienese.

It is a horse race, but only on the surface.

In my first book, *Seasons in Tuscany*, I described the *contrade* system of town districts, great extended families that draw fierce loyalties from the people who live within their confines. They are ghettos of passion. The Palio is the fiercest manifestation of this *contrade* system. It is one of the most famous horse races in the world, certainly one of the most historic. It takes place in one of the world's great outdoor arenas, the majestic, scallop-shaped expanse of Siena's main piazza, Il Campo. It is watched live on television by millions. But this is as nothing to the Sienese. Twice a year for those brief seconds, their honour, their pride, their soul is at stake.

The drive from San Clemente to Siena takes about an hour. It is also one that takes me back thousands of years, to the earliest years of 'civilised' Europe. Siena, the old town, sits on three hills. Legend records that it was founded by Senius, the son of Remus, who was one of the twin founders of the Eternal City some three hours to the south. Today statues of the suckling vixen stand proudly in piazzas around the old town.

The Etruscans were here centuries before the birth of Christ. So, too, were the Imperial Romans. Siena was the seat of one of the many separate city-states that dominated Italian life through the centuries. It was less than two hundred years ago that Italy became a single unified country; the regional heritage still lingers in dialect, customs and food. Siena fought bitterly with the power of Florence, *Firenze*, to the north before achieving a famous victory over its rivals in 1260. Nearly a century later the Black Death ravaged the medieval city killing three in every four of its citizens. The first bank was founded in what is now the nation of Italy—the offices still stand today, an imposing grey-stoned building in the Piazza Salimbeni. Siena finally became part of the Grand Duchy of Tuscany in 1559. It has a noble history and a proud one. And there is no prouder reflection of the Sienese sense of their history than the *contrade*, the seventeen districts of the city. The *contrade* of a town or city are the essence, the driving force, of a Tuscan's relationship to his or her surroundings. The family is all, but your *contrada* is your extended family. Each *contrada* has its own symbol, flag, colours, traditions and rules. You will have your newborn child baptised from the waters of the *contrada* fountain after the church ceremony. You will be married in the *contrada* church. In past centuries, the young men would have marched to war under their *contrada* colours. Today, you march through the streets under the flying, twirling flags of your *alfieri* (flag wavers) and to the beat of your *tamburini* (drummers) on the saint day of your *contrada*. On that same day, as you come back to your *contrada* territory with your fellow members, you will perform the *rientro*, thus showing your annual renewal of *appartenenza*, allegiance.

But your mind will always be tuned to the two days in summer, 2 July and 16 August, which are the days of the Palio.

It has been held in many guises over seven centuries—buffalo races, bullfights, soccer contests, float parades through the streets of the city, even fist fights. One such fight attracted more than a thousand pugilists and left a casualty list of four dead and an unrecorded number of broken noses; these affairs were promptly banned by the civic authorities.

Dukes, kings, emperors and a host of other worthies have witnessed the Palio over the ages. Even convicted criminals used to be released from prison in August to take part in the pre- and after-match functions.

The second of the two annual Palios, on 16 August, is dedicated to the patron saint of the city. The first, on 2 July, has a reputedly miraculous origin. Popular history records that on 2 July 1594, a duty guard in the town district named after Provenzano Salvani, who defeated the Florentine invaders at the Battle of Monteparti, took a drunken dislike to a small statue of the Madonna di Provenzano in the area. He decided to blow it away, but succeeded only in blowing himself away when his arquebus exploded. The statue was damaged, but the Sienese decided that this was still a miracle and built a temple to house it. Some sixty years later, the day dedicated to the 'miracle' and the visitation by the Virgin Mary who caused it became an official Palio race day.

Virtually every town in Tuscany has its version of the Palio, a contest between the *contrade*. Montepulciano has its barrel race, Foiano della Chiana its floats, Torrita di Siena its donkey race. They are fiercely fought with much honour and pride riding on the outcome. Like the Sienese *contrade*, each district hangs banners, emblems bearing its colours as 'race day' nears. *Contrade* members sport scarves bearing their banner and colours around their necks, over their shoulders, tied to their belts or looped through handbag straps.

It would be easy to describe the Palio as merely one more manifestation of this *contrade* rivalry. The Palio is the Everest, the peak of it all. There are seventeen *contrade* in Siena. Each has its own name, motto and symbolism: Contrada Tarturuga (Tortoise, 'I harbour strength and perseverance', steadfastness); Aquila (Eagle, 'Of the eagle, the beak, the talon and the wing', pugnacity); Pantera (the panther, 'The Panther roared and the people awoke', audacity); Drago (the dragon, 'The ardour in my heart becomes flame in my mouth', ardour). These are passionate descriptors, as passionate as the vividness of the *contrade* colours—reds, greens, yellows, blues, purples, crimson, orange . . . all boldly luminescent, proclaiming that each *contrada* is the proudest.

In past centuries, the *contrade* were numbered by the score. The plague put paid to many of those. The total waxed and waned over the centuries until 1723, when the current seventeen became entrenched.

Only ten of the seventeen *contrade* contest each Palio for safety reasons. The packed earth course around the perimeter of the piazza is narrow and the corners tight; two—San Martino and Casato—are virtual right angles. The former has mattresses installed on its outer fence for protection when jockeys fall, as is often the case. Broken limbs are an accepted risk for the honour of riding in the Palio.

The ten competing *contrade* include the seven who did not ride in the equivalent race the previous year. They race as of right. The remaining three are drawn by lot in Il Campo. This is a tense moment for the *contrade* not in the race as of right. On the draw rests their hopes of victory. The ceremony draws thousands of *contradaioli*, *contrade* members. The selection for the 2 July race is made on the last Sunday in May, and the first or second Sunday in July for the 16 August race.

Thus it might be that a *contrada* may race in only one of that year's events. At best, it may be in both. The very worst is if it misses out completely.

The selection completed, the coming Palio becomes a consuming issue throughout Siena.

The Palio is no classic on the international racing calendar. It lacks the finery of a Kentucky Derby or the elegance of an Epsom Derby. It certainly carries no big prize money of a Prix de L'Arc de Triomphe. The jockeys are not lean and lithe like those who ride in the Melbourne Cup or on Cheltenham Cup day. They are squat and peasant-like. Their eyes glower with rustic cunning and their faces glow with the rough treatment of the elements. They are not a pretty lot.

But they are hardened. The rigour of those short seconds on the packed dirt circumference demands a special toughness and strength. The concussion from the surface, the power of the horse, the tightness of the track's turns, the frenzy of the crowd, the looming buildings, the incredible demands of those right-angled corners . . . it is strength not agility, guts not grace that will carry away the banner.

They come from a harsh environment—the searing heat and rugged hills of Sicily, the storms and marshes of Maremma. That breeds the resilience that the Palio demands; the soft and feminine hills of the Siena countryside could not give these jockeys the explosive power and strength they need for those seventy-five seconds of release. They are the Visigoths of the racetrack.

Each *contrada* employs its own jockey, so they are known quantities. Their skills, track record, strengths and weaknesses are understood and a *contrada* will hire a jockey based on these. He is theirs. The horse he will race—and on whose back the hopes of the *contrada* will also ride—adds a special zest to the Palio as it is chosen by the fates.

Months before the Palio the horse owners offer animals for consideration as Palio competitors. There is only a modest purse at the end for the winner, one that in no way can compensate for the cost of raising such an animal. The owners are motivated more by vanity, the honour of raising a Palio winner, because it is the carrier of the dreams of each competing *contrada*.

Up to thirty horses are offered to the organisation that oversees the administration and running of the Palio. From these, the captains of the *contrada* will choose ten after a series of trials, or *tratte*.

Experts—experienced and amateur alike—follow the *tratte* intensely. From these ranks, there will be a winner. It is the animals that bring the real nobility to the Palio—not the nobility of the thoroughbred's bloodline and certainly not a prancing elegance. Rather, it is the nobility of a proud fighter. That is the overriding quality these men (and in Tuscan society, there can be no question that such crucial assessments and decisions could be anything but male ones) look for with their practised eyes. Yet there are other qualities needed, too, that the *tratte* are intended to reveal.

Some are quantifiable. Does it come from a bloodline of stamina and strength? Has it raced in the Palio before? If so, how did it run? How did it cope with the track, the corners, the crowd, the building-enclosed arena? What physical shape is it in? Does it have a history of injury?

But the crucial tests are less definable. Does it have a weakness on its right that will hinder it on the right-hand track? Does it have extra power on its right to withstand the stresses of those two cruel right-angle turns? Will it falter at them? Does it have strength, speed, stamina? And then there are questions of its mental strengths. Does it have the fire of the spirit of a competitor in its eye? Does it have the fire of courage in its belly? Does it want to win?

After each trial, the captain of the *contrada* will report back to his 'team' with such observations he has gleaned about these questions. Gradually the trials will cull out all but the ten horses everyone can accept for the race. It's a tricky decision with many considerations.

Finally, the captains of the *contrade* meet to select the ten horses that will race. It is an agreed decision, but uncertainties still remain. No one yet knows who the remaining three *contrade* will be. More importantly, they have no idea of what horse will carry them to victory, failure, or worst, defeat by the particular enemy of your *contrada*. This is the essence of the race. *Contrada* life continues throughout the year with feast days, baptisms, outings, games, preparations, the training of the young drummer boys, dinners, meetings . . . but the Palio proper begins with the selection of the ten horses.

The intelligence reports on the trials by the captains circulate quickly throughout the *contrade*. News of each horse's condition, prowess, fitness, spreads through the narrow streets. Everyone becomes an instant armchair expert as they discuss the merits and defects of the trial horses.

It would be easy to compare it to the build-up before an international rugby test or an event like the Superbowl. But it is more elemental than that and a comparison with a major high school or university contest is more accurate. The Palio is not just a race. It combines pride, history, tradition and a sense of family; a way of life that goes to the starting line each year.

The Palio in earnest begins four days before race day. The jockeys have been hired, the artist has completed the banner, the packed dirt track has been laid and the grandstands are in place. As long ago as a month or so, the three *contrade* not competing as of right were drawn by lot; the *contrade* field is known, though the horses representing them are not. Now comes the absolutely crucial moment when each horse is assigned by lot to the competing *contrade*.

Tension is high as thousands gather in Il Campo for the drawing by lot. First, a numbered ball is drawn from one urn corresponding to a horse, then, from a second urn, another ball representing the *contrada* it will ride for. There are groans of despair, cheers of good fortune as each horse—its qualities now well known—are matched to each *contrada*.

As each draw is completed a *contrada* handler leads the

assigned horse away for stabling. It will be cosseted, groomed and closely guarded, to avoid 'nobbling'.

To have a *brenna*, a nag, plucked from the draw is bad news. Italians are a very superstitious people and on the morning of the draw many Sienese will seek good fortune from omens or fortune-tellers. The horse and jockeys now matched, a series of *prove*, trials, takes place in the piazza. This gives the jockeys a chance to test both horse and course, to assess the horses' reactions to and abilities around the circle, the trickiness of the course and their own strategies for running it.

On the eve of the race, Siena becomes one vast outdoor restaurant as each *contrada* holds a traditional dress rehearsal dinner. Depending on the population of the *contrada*, hundreds or more than a thousand will sit down in a *contrada* piazza or street. Songs, speeches, hopes, fears are the order of the night— and, of course, eating and drinking. One estimate suggests that as many as 25,000 people dine *al fresco* in Siena on the evening before race day.

Contrade have alliances with others. But of overriding importance are the enmities that some share—fierce rivalries that go back centuries over some slight or other. Murders and fights, songs that ridicule, vulgar gestures—if the *contrada* is your soul, hatred of the enemy is your heart. In the race itself if your *contrada* is not competing, you cheer on your allies to beat your enemy.

The banner of each *contrada* or 'rag' as it is known to locals, is a cloth banner about two metres tall and over half a metre wide. Artists are specially commissioned to create it for each race. It always features a representation of the Virgin Mary at its top (a modern artist courted controversy by depicting her as a mother with a baby's pram). The winning *contrada* also receives silver replicas of the old *talleri*, coins.

Such is the Palio's importance to the city that only a handful of the more than six hundred run since the 17th century have been called off—a cholera epidemic, the two world wars, a king's assassination, an earthquake . . . *straordinario* or extra Palios are also as scarce as an Italian without a cellphone. The six hundredth anniversary of the birth of Siena's patron saint, St Catherine, called for one in 1947. So too did the first landing on the moon in 1969. And the millennium year, 2000, was occasion for another *straordinario*.

My first encounter with the fervour of the Palio began in 1998, twelve months before my year of the Palio, 1999. It was to be only a fleeting glimpse, but a revealing one that demonstrated quite clearly the passions involved.

When I first discovered that my new Tuscan home was so close to Siena, I resolved to experience this piece of history. Better still would be to write about it. I decided that my approach to the Palio would be through the eyes of one *contrada*; to contact each of the full seventeen would be too daunting with my very limited Italian language.

My first approach was to the Siena tourist office. The one that most tourists find is in Il Campo itself. As I walked past the opening that leads down into Il Campo, dodging pedestrians and vehicles, I knew what I wanted from my *contrada*-to-be. It had to be one that was competing in both Palios that year; two chances at victory were better odds than one. I preferred one that was strictly confined within the old town walls; as Siena has grown, its population had naturally expanded beyond the confines of the old town, tumbling down the hills it was founded on and into the countryside below. My *contrada* was to be clearly associated with historic Siena.

I knew those were my terms. But I didn't know if they could be met. I was, I know, being presumptuous—a *straniero* without the language and without a complete knowledge of what it meant to be a *contrada* member. People were born, baptised and married in their *contrada*. They even took it to death with them, the headstones on their graves bearing their *contrada* emblem.

But you have to start somewhere. And my first tentative inquiry was at the desk of Signorina Benci in the office of the Siena tourist association.

It was also my initiation into the *contrade* rivalries. As we sat at Signorina Benci's desk, she began checking for double-header *contrade* for that year.

Pantera, the panther was one of the very few. At this her colleague, a young woman, snorted and made a brief comment in Italian from her desk behind me. 'She says she doesn't like Pantera,' Signorina Benci translated. I had obviously been quickly consigned to the *contrada* scrapheap. She gave me the name of a Pantera contact. As I got up to leave, she noted that no one in the tourist office was a Pantera member. 'We have Sea-snail, I am Wave, there's even a Tower.'

I decided to experience a Palio to get a 'feel' for the emotion and excitement before contacting my Pantera number; my lack of Italian was also a daunting prospect.

In the event, I saw neither race. The second of July was blisteringly hot and the prospect of standing in Il Campo with thousands of people for hours while the Tuscan sun radiated from the brick buildings surrounding it was too grim to face. In August, Nancy and I were also preparing to return to New Jersey to be married.

My first year of Palio thus never reached the starting line.

But I was better prepared for Palio Year Two. I had a plan, I had contacts. And I had a new *contrada*.

Civetta, the owl, fulfilled my objectives: it was running in both Palios of 1999; it was in the old town (even better, it abutted Il Campo and was the *contrada* of our favourite hang-out in the city, Bar Centrale) and had strong historical associations with both Siena and the *contrade* system. Also, it had not won a Palio for twenty years. Perhaps its time was due. The Contrada Priorale of Civetta lies in the very heart of the city. It is one of the smallest *contrade* with barely 700 members. Its southern boundary is marked by one end of the Via di Città, which runs into the street named Banchi di Sotto. Beyond the buildings on the southern side of these streets lies Il Campo—a vast expanse as you emerge from the confines of the streets. From there it spreads north through narrow dark cobblestoned streets lined with glowering medieval buildings. At best its boundaries are only a few hundred metres across. You can almost smell the history emanating from the buildings and feel it brushing your face as it wafts through the streets. The atmosphere has a brooding quality, one that whispers of plagues and wars and intrigues—of loss rather than gain.

Not all *contrade* have additions to their title such as 'Priorale'. These are honours bestowed for particular services or deeds. Aquila (Eagle) is the 'Noble Contrada of Aquila', thanks to the warm welcome it gave the visiting Emperor Charles V nearly 500 years ago. The hospitality was such that he awarded the title in gratitude. The Captain Contrada of Onda (Wave) recognises its role as the supplier of troops to guard the Palazzo Pubblico, seat of the old Republic of Siena, which still is in use as the town hall today—marked by the distinctive tower that stands, like the Duomo, high above the city skyline.

Some titles are of more recent vintage. Victor Emmanuel III granted Giraffa (Giraffe) the title of 'Imperial' after its July 1936, Palio victory; the race was dedicated to 'the Italian Empire in East Africa'. As recently as 1980, Istrice (Porcupine) earned the right to be known as the 'Sovereign Contrada of Istrice' a title bestowed by the Sovereign Military Order of Malta because the Order had its headquarters nearby in the 14th century.

Civetta earned its 'Priorale' title after hosting the inaugural meeting of all the Priors (heads or presidents) of the seventeen *contrade* that exist today. Its symbol, the owl, reputedly derives from the goddess Minerva, who regarded the bird as sacred. It is claimed that a temple dedicated to the goddess once stood on the territory of the *contrada*. Its heraldic symbol reflects its name—a crowned owl perched on a branch. The bird is flanked by two letters recognising associations with historical figures : 'U' (Umberto I) and 'M' (Margherita), both of Savoy. Its colours are claret red and black (in equal parts) and with white stripes, frets and arabesques as adornments. Its motto is 'I see in the night' and it symbolises shrewdness and astuteness.

Civetta has its own historic places, too, from which decisions emerged that reverberated throughout the land that is now the one nation of Italy and, like waves in a pond, across the continent. The Consiglio dei Reggitori (the ruling council of the Republic of Siena) met in ancient Chiesa di San Cristoforo, the Church of Saint Christopher. In 1260, the council decided to make war against Florence, resulting in the victory of Montaperti. The victory is still commemorated today by the tall pillar in the Piazza Tolomei in front of the church. Behind the church is the palace of the enormously powerful Tolomei family.

Two streets run past each side of San Cristoforo. The right-hand one is Via Cecco Angiolieri, named after the poet who was born and lived in it between 1258 and 1312. It is a curved street that slowly descends past the blue-neon sign outside our Bar Centrale, towards the Seat, headquarters of the *contrada*. Where the street (and it is more an alley than a street) reaches a brief plateau, a short climb to the left takes us up to the small piazza where the Castellare degli Ugurgieri lines the back wall. To call it a piazza suggests a grandness that it does not merit physically; it is little more than a large courtyard perhaps the size of a tennis court. The fortified palace, the seat of the *contrada*, dates back to the 13th century and was the home of Giovanni Ugurgieri, who was a leader of the Sienese military companies that achieved victory and fame on the battlefield of Montaperti.

Civetta has, therefore, an illustrious history as a *contrada*. No less illustrious is its history with the Palio. It won the first Palio to be run between the *contrade*, in 1581. Nearly two hundred years later, in 1757, it was the first *contrada* to win both Palios in the same year—a feat known as the *cappotto* or hat trick. In modern days, the feat was last achieved (by Tartaruga, the Tortoise) in 1953.

But for now it languishes without receiving the Palio banner, the 'rag', for twenty long years. In fact, since the race was revived after World War Two, it has won only six of more than one hundred and twenty Palios. Its young folk, born, baptised and initiated into the fervour of both the *contrada* and the Palio, have never known the ecstasy that follows a Palio victory. The tears they have shed have not been of joy but frustration and sorrow.

They have not experienced a victory march through the streets nor the celebration of the victory dinner in the floodlit Il Campo. They wait, they hope, they pray, they look for omens, they fortify each other with confidence—like the old people who yearn for that thrilling moment experienced so many years ago.

The *contrade* system guards its property, the Palio, zealously. It once sued a multinational that markets one of those mineral-rich athletic drinks when it used an unauthorised photograph of the Palio in its advertising. This intelligence came to me from Silvia Matteoli, the young and efficient 'Girl Friday' of the Consorzio per la Tutela del Palio di Siena, the *contrade* consortium that promotes and protects the Palio culture.

Like a one-man version of that multinational, I was to learn just how fiercely and assiduously the Consorzio protects its image. It is an increasing headache for Siena, this fight to protect the race. While Siena embraces the Palio with fire, outsiders threaten to quell the flames of passion. Animal rights activists—as militant as any death-or-glory fighters—have become shriller in their cries to end the race. And anyone who knows the dangers of the race—except, of course, the Sienese—will acknowledge their arguments have some merit. Il Campo is a killer course. In the ten Palios before I forayed into it, the treacherous curves and sharp right angles had resulted in injuries so severe that five horses had to be destroyed. The toll on the human participants—the jockeys—is also severe, although not so deadly . . . broken legs, shoulders and arms from falls, particularly at the venomous turns of San Martino and Casato.

The city has made some concessions to the increasing protests of barbarity. New rubber barriers were installed on the outside curve of San Martino in my Year of Civetta; the material is used in Formula One motor racing. And a new blood testing regime with a list of prohibited substances was established in the same year.

But these seem to be cosmetic changes at best, a sop to the voices of protest. Violations of the drug system do not result in disqualification and test results will only 'go public' if there is an investigation into an accident.

The Sienese maintain that new measures like the barriers and the tests were decided by the city itself and not as a result of outside protests. And when a court fined two important members of a *contrada* after excessive levels of a dangerous drug were found in a horse that had to be destroyed, the city itself paid the fines and appealed the sentence as a symbol that the Palio is Siena itself.

'The city decided to oppose this sentence because we don't want to establish a precedent,' explained the Mayor's spokesman in a newspaper interview. He also dismissed the animal rights protests as 'stupid', claiming that accidents were part of any sport and the Palio was unfairly fingered. 'Some people claim that of all the horse races in the world, this is the worst. It's not true. It's just that this is the most celebrated.'

The door allowing entry to the *contrada* system opened for me a month later. The Priora or president of Civetta had agreed to meet me to discuss my proposal, Silvia Matteoli announced. 'I suggest we meet here at the consortium offices as he doesn't speak English and I can translate.' We agreed a time and date and Nancy and I, duly scrubbed and polished, arrived to meet Dottor Luca Garosi.

Well-bred continental European men have an elegance of character that in my experience is unmatched. The English gentleman tries but is too pompous in the effort; the English nobility have been inbred for so long they have lost all elegance. The American, of course, have neither the heritage nor the tradition to give them the strength required—only the money, which is hardly a determining factor. New Zealanders simply don't enter the equation. The European man of class and distinction has it all—grace, charm, manners, elegance, the ease of self-confidence and culture without the need to wear it on his sleeve, a knowledge and acceptance of a world beyond his borders. He is a man to be admired.

Dottor Garosi lacked English (we later discovered he knew *un poco*, a little, but like most Italians was embarrassed to reveal it), but he had all the other characteristics of a gentleman—refined, genteel, gracious, with that certain ease of posture, education, civility, a quiet wit, warm eyes and impeccable clothing of a man of honour. I supposed these are all required attributes if you are to be the chief representative of a Sienese *contrada*, with its expectations of loyalty, duty, devotion and sense of heritage.

We began our meeting in a small, coffin-like room without windows. Later, after explaining my mission, we walked into the large, airy, light but austere conference room where a long wooden table glowed like the sun. Dottor Garosi showed me the Civetta confines on a map of Siena; later still, he drew the boundaries on one of the give-away maps that the tourist office distributes to lost souls seeking a direction to their short Siena life.

I seemed to pass muster for he agreed to my proposal, or at least to give it a go. We would meet one evening in the week preceding the race so I could watch one of the *prove*, trials, in Il Campo. He would also arrange someone who could act as a translator.

As we parted over shaken hands, I offered, 'This year we win,' more in a gesture of solidarity than expectation.

He waved his hands as if to say '*Forse, forse,*' perhaps, perhaps.

'*Due volte,* two times,' I said.

'To win once is good enough.'

I know little of the mysteries of horseflesh—the breeding, the conditioning, the 'form'; I am like those people who place a bet on the basis that I liked the horse's colour.

But I did want to experience one of the six *prove* that precede the Palio itself. These are, in themselves, meaningless—a chance for horse, jockey and course to get to know each other. But they involve much ceremony and bravado for each *contrada*; it was also an opportunity to meet with Dottor Garosi again and to discover the heartbeat of Civetta.

Nancy and I parked in one of the little side streets in the posh part of Siena, outside the old town but still home to old blood and, one suspects, new money. As we continued into the town centre and Civetta, past souvenir shops that co-existed with a tiny grocery store and another lingerie shop, there was ample evidence that this part of our journey was deep in Oca territory, the home of the Goose. Ceramic busts of a goose's head in the white, green and red *contrada* colours jutted from high up on the walls of the buildings. Banners, too, hung limply in the wilting summer heat. Oca has an illustrious *contrada* and Palio history. Saint Catherine of Siena, the city's patron saint, was born within its confines. And it has carried away the Palio banner more times than any other *contrada*—eleven since the racing resumed after the war.

At normal times of the year, *contrade* colours are modestly displayed. But this was not a normal time of the year; the streets and citizens were bedecked with the colours. It was obvious when we passed from Oca territory into Civetta's district. The colours lining the Banchi di Sopra changed from the Goose's to the claret, black and white of Civetta. And here we had an appointment with Dottor Garosi at his headquarters.

Down the *via*, around the curve, perhaps three hundred metres, a little more, and at the intersection of streets, the *contrada* members are gathering. To the left, the short alley leads up to the tiny piazza which houses the nerve centre of Civetta. To the right, another short street leads down to the arena, the concourse, the *corsa*, Il Campo. But for now the *contradaioli* gather in the intersection itself. Against one wall of buildings is a stall selling beer, wine, nibbles and other snacks. Old people have brought the ubiquitous white plastic outdoor chairs that cover restaurant floors, *terrazze* and swimming pool surrounds throughout this part of Italy, probably throughout the country. Young men and women lounge against the walls of the buildings. The middle-aged gather in conclaves, no doubt discussing the prospects of the *prova* and the Palio itself. There is a definite tension, a subdued and hushed subtlety in the air that reveals to me perhaps my first under-standing that this is serious business.

Dottor Garosi is there—elegant, formal, correct and imposing. He explains that he has arranged for some English speakers to help answer my questions. Shortly he introduces us to Agata and Giuseppe and to our education into the mystique of the Palio and the pride of the *contrade* system.

Ironically, Agata is not Sienese, Tuscan or even Italian. She is originally from Hungary. But she now shares her life with Giuseppe in Siena, where, remarkably, she did her university thesis on the Palio. She also teaches English to Italians.

Neither is Giuseppe from Siena, but his mother was born in the Civetta boundaries. So Civetta he is. He is tall and thin; she is short and has those Slavic eyes that promise an impassioned temperament.

Through them, we learn that the Priora is a law lecturer at Siena University. He was born in the *contrada* district but now lives outside it. Each *contrada* elects a president for two years, and Dottor Garosi's term began just two months before our first meeting.

He explains Civetta's main liability, its small size.

'It is in the centre of the city; there are many offices, banks, commerce so not many people living here. Apartments are hard to find and very expensive.'

From both the Priora and Giuseppe, I begin to understand the rivalry against the adversary *contrada*, in Civetta's case Liocorno, the Unicorn. One of Liocorno's boundaries directly abuts Civetta's headquarters.

'The next-door *contrada* is the enemy,' explains Dottor Garosi. 'For the *contrada*, the Palio is a war,' he adds, pointing his two index fingers at each other in a head-on confrontation gesture.

'The enemy is the main thing. You must beat him,' says Giuseppe. 'You never want him to win. If you [your *contrada*] is not running, you hope one of your allies will beat him.'

Civetta's allies are Aquila (Eagle), Istrice (Porcupine), Giraffa (Giraffe) and Pantera (Panther). The enmity with Liocorno is relatively recent in Palio terms. It began in 1954, said Giuseppe later, when the Unicorn won and began singing songs mocking its rival Civetta—' a question of territory'.

'Sometimes there are fights, sometimes we look at each other with faces. Some years these are more frequent, even twice in the year [if both are running in each Palio], sometimes only every five years or so.'

Gradually the *contradaioli* have gathered as the time for that evening's *prova* has neared. The trial is timed for 7.45 and about thirty minutes beforehand the *contrada* horse is brought out of the stables where it has been cosseted and guarded since the selection day. It is taken into a roped-off area outside the *contrada* headquarters where it is paraded and admired; in these days of the Palio, the horse becomes god-like. On it all hopes ride, all fears dwell. This July, the god is the five-year-old Lupo del Cimino. It is its first Palio and it is not regarded highly. The jockey is Mario Canu but Civetta regard for him is also luke-warm even though they chose him; other jockeys have better reputations. Siena itself has already determined the favourites— Drago (Dragon) for the horse, Pantera (Panther) for the jockey.

But the young folk of Civetta, those who have never experienced a Palio win in their brief lives, have shown obstinate and admirable faith—and good humour—in their horse and jockey. A common sign on Italian gates is *Attenti al cane*, beware of the dog. They have bought up stocks of these signs and, with a felt-tip pen, changed '*cane*' to 'Canu', the name of their jockey. Above it they have also added the name of the horse, Lupo, which means 'wolf' in Italian. These signs they wear draped around their necks. It's a fine play on words, for which the Tuscans are famous.

Curiously, the *prove* in the few days preceding the Palio provide the *contradaioli* with a better opportunity to demonstrate their honour and loyalty than the race itself. On race day, it is a haphazard crush of thousands of people in the centre of Il Campo. Locals and tourists jostle for position, friends become separated, isolated pockets of a particular *contradaioli* stand alongside those from other *contrade*. It's a bit of a dog-eat-dog occasion. Some *contrade* hire a section of the tiered seating that surrounds the outside of the course, tucked up against the ancient buildings that have looked silently down on the race for so many centuries. But this seating is expensive and those who can afford it are not the sort to indulge in singing and flag-waving.

There is also a solemnity and tension on race day. It is a time for tradition, rituals, respect and reflection.

A *prova* is a different matter. There is nothing hanging on the outcome of the trial. The large crowd of race day will not be gathered in the piazza. People are still at work.

While an important part of the Palio ritual, then, the *prove* give each *contrada* a chance to strut its collective stuff.

Gradually, those *contrada* members who are able begin to gather by their headquarters. Old women sit with all the stoicism of old Italian women in chairs, while younger ones work in a kitchen area on one side of the tiny Civetta piazza; a section of the piazza has been roped off—the horse that will carry Civetta's hopes in the coming race will be paraded here soon. Old men stand in groups, perhaps discussing past Palios, reviving memories of the last Civetta win they witnessed twenty years ago. Young men and women flirt in the way that all young men and women do—self-consciously and with nervous laughs. Children run around and past the 'grown-ups'. *Contrada* officials like Dottor Garosi look important in beautifully-cut suits and silk ties. Civetta banners hang from window balconies.

In the distance, singing and chanting begins to get louder as other *contrade* further from Il Campo march towards the arena; Civetta will be one of the last to head off as it is so close to the piazza.

Finally, after the sleekly groomed horse has been paraded, it is led to the top of a short, narrow street leading down to the amphitheatre. At the bottom, another *contrada* is passing, the singing and chanting of its own songs booming up towards the waiting Civetta.

There is a strict order of parade. The horse is in front. Behind gather the leaders, then the menfolk and, lastly, the women and children. Some things never change in Tuscany.

At last, the parade begins to move down the street, more a lane really. As it moves out, the marchers behind the dignified leaders begin to sing and chant their Civetta songs and slogans. These are voices lusty and loud with passion. The street is like an amplifying chamber and the noise of the advancing crowd booms down it. My Hungarian Palio tutor Agata had explained that the first song is always against the *contrada* enemy, in this case Liocorno. Some songs and chants are traditional, others are created for a particular Palio, still others are changed or invented between *prove*.

Banners are held high above the parade and fists are flung proudly into the air to emphasise the singing. The young men march like warriors, their voices overpowering in their strength of commitment and honour. They are marching to battle, to the drums of a centuries-old war.

There is a brief dogleg at the bottom, then a turn into the short street leading under an arch into Il Campo. The horse has been taken off to join the other entries in the courtyard by the town hall before emerging into the arena for this evening's *prova*. We enter first, under the arch and into an exploding world of colour and chanting and banners and fists punching the air.

It is an extraordinary atmosphere. The *contrade* have all gathered from around the city, each determined to show their pride in being the strongest, their honour the greatest. They stand in the centre area or gather on the stands, each driven to outdo the others.

It reminds me of what the atmosphere must be like at an FA Cup Final in London's Wembley Stadium. Except here there are seventeen sets of cheering fans, not two.

After about thirty minutes, the ten mounted horses contesting this coming Palio emerge and trot up the slope and around to the rope of the starting line. At the drop of the rope, the jockeys begin their three laps of testing the horse and the course. Some lope, others gallop; it does not have the drama of a real race but that is not the point. It certainly doesn't diminish the cheering.

The trial over, the horses disappear back into the courtyard and the *contrade* members regroup to march back to their respective headquarters, their singing as loud as ever as they disperse.

'And this is just the trial?' a bemused American tourist asks her husband.

Ibrahim, the black African, was nonplussed.

The day before, the young Catholic priest had been tending his flock under the blazing sun in a dusty Nigerian village. Just hours before he had emerged into the chaos of an international airport in Rome, then faced a 200-kilometre drive along a hectic Italian motorway. And now he sat at a table under the stars of a Tuscan night, surrounded by medieval buildings and hundreds of Sienese diners, washing down antipasti and ravioli and roast meats with the robust red wine that continuously emerged from some mysterious cellar.

He was jet-lagged and culture-shocked and I felt sorry for him.

'Are you enjoying it?' I asked him solicitously.

'I don't like this sort of thing,' he said morosely. It was clear that all he wanted to do was to be in bed or, better, back in his Nigerian village, humble—and safe—in his own environment. If he had been Italian he would no doubt have likened it to a scene from Dante. Instead, he had had the ill luck to time his study tour to Siena to coincide with the final big event of the lead-up to the day of the Palio. Even worse, the Italian Catholic priest assigned to help him settle in had insisted on dragging him to it. The Italian Father was quite oblivious to the state of his young charge; this was Siena, this was the spirit of the Palio and this was the *cena propiziatoria*, the proprietary dinner—the eve-of-race 'dress rehearsal dinner'. How could anyone not be caught up in it?

How, indeed? On the night before each Palio, Siena becomes a huge outdoor dinner party as each of the seventeen *contrade*— even those not in tomorrow's race—hold an open-air feast in their respective territories. I had dutifully paid my 60,000 lire to join the dinner of my new Civetta *contrada*. My ticket number was 770; considering Civetta is one of the smallest *contrade* with just 700 members, it was clear that the dinners are open to others—guests (Ibrahim), outsiders (myself) and even tourists—prepared to pay.

The Civetta dinner was in the Piazza Tolomei. A grand, larger-than-life statue of a member of that illustrious Sienese family stands rather haughtily in the centre, bird droppings running from his Renaissance cloth hat and cape-draped shoulders. Nancy had left for a visit to family and friends back in New Jersey so I was on my own as I walked into the *centro storico*, the historical centre, of the city in the early evening. I joined the gathering diners at what was the obvious pre-dinner meeting place at the bottom of the street leading up to the piazza. People milled about, draped with the Civetta colours as they waited for the time to walk up the street to the dinner. Some of the younger ones had come with two blow-up plastic dogs, one with a Civetta scarf and one with the colours of the enemy, Liocorno. These were positioned on the cobblestones in a doggy sexual position; no prizes for guessing which was on top.

The dinner was a curious cocktail of intense and varied emotion—sombre, dignified, nervous, tense, hushed, and outright rowdy. The sombreness came from the older diners, the dignity from the top table of officials and important people sitting in elevated isolation in a line along the front of the church facing one side of the piazza. There was a tense hush in the air where the more mature and elegant members of the *contrada* sat at the white-covered trestle tables, reflecting on hopes of the morrow. The rowdiness came from the warriors, the young males and females who had been placed at one long table in the centre of the crowd. It seemed to be a strategic placement as they provided the evening's entertainment.

The affair was so big, the tables so many, that the *contrada* had been forced to commandeer seating space in the street that ran across the back end of the piazza. As No. 770 in the seating arrangements, I was relegated to this area. The street was blocked off at either end by a wooden fence. Curious and bemused tourists on their post-dinner evening stroll stopped to stare at the scene.

At around 11 p.m. there were a few speeches, mercifully and sensibly short, to fire up the crowd with *contrada* patriotism. They certainly revved up the young warriors. By now the endless flow of wine was making itself felt; the songs were louder and lustier, the arm punching in the air stronger and risk of damage to the chairs much greater as they were turned into performance platforms.

The wine was, of course, essential to the event. So too was the dinner. It is simply impossible to conceive of any Italian social activity not featuring food and wine; it would be like Mass without a prayer, a forest without trees. The eve-of-Palio dinner was no exception. And, as usual, it followed the standard ritual of dining in Tuscany: an antipasto of *prosciutto crudo*, two *primi*—risotto and ravioli—and a *secondo* of roast beef.

Across the table was a couple from Siena, but from a different *contrada*. They were there as guests of another couple of Civetta *contradaioli*.

The husband explained that it was okay to attend the dinner of another *contrada*—as long as it was not your enemy.

'I wouldn't ever come to an enemy dinner even if I was invited by my best friend. No one would,' he said with conviction.

On Palio days, he added, a husband and wife who come from different *contrade* would often spend the day apart, each at their own headquarters.

'Their children may even be sent to a neutral *contrada* for the day.'

Later, I walked across to say goodnight to Agata and Giuseppe. It was around midnight and although the party was clearly just warming up, I had an hour's drive back to San Clemente.

'I think there may be some fighting tonight,' said Agata. 'The Civetta men have been singing all the time against Unicorn but Unicorn has stayed quiet. Maybe there are police on site where the boundary is.'

Such is the emotion of the Palio.

It was a pleasant, warm summer's evening in Tuscany. The real heat would come tomorrow.

The day of my first Palio was an egg-fryer—a scorching sun by 7.30, corpse-still air and the deep, deep blue of the Tuscan sky.

Sensibly I chose the hottest part of the day—early afternoon—to drive to Siena! If I had taken a leg of lamb in the car it would have been nicely roasted by the time I reached the city.

Siena was awash with sound and colour. *Contradaioli* marched through the streets singing their particular war chants, people paraded themselves and their colours, banners hung from every building, streetlight and shop awning. There seemed to be more flags on show than on Memorial Day in America. Young children waved flags aloft, men wore them like bullet belts over their shoulders, women were smartly turned out in dresses of their *contrada* colours, the young warriors' faces were coated with war paint of their colours. Even the tourists who flocked to Siena in their thousands were part of the action. Siena was in Palio mode—and dressed up for the occasion.

If there was excitement and buzz in the air and in the streets, it was a completely different atmosphere at Civetta headquarters. *Contradaioli* sat or stood in hushed little groups as they contemplated the odds for the coming race. The tension was so dense I could have cut out a piece and taken it back to San Clemente to grow.

Slowly, those taking part in the pre-race parade began to gather in the narrow street, dressed in their period costumes, some on horseback, others armed with fearsome weapons of old. The Corteo Storico or historical parade around Il Campo before the race is a highly ritualised affair dating back to the early 19th century: mace bearers; commanders; drummers; trumpeters; standard bearers; representatives from other towns like Montalcino who once supported the old Republic of Siena in its wars against archenemy Florence; others representing the Thirds (the three main territories in the city; Sienese nobles, academes from the university, and representatives of the city's various trades guilds; a team from each of the seventeen *contrade* and, finally, aloft on an oxen-drawn war chariot, the banner for that race and the Balzana, the black and white pennant of Siena.

In mid-afternoon, the bell in the Mangia tower of the town hall rings. It's a signal for the *contrade* to gather for the parade and race. But first each horse and its jockey competing in that day's race go into the their respective *contrade* churches. There, the priest blesses both, urging them, 'Go, and return as a winner,' a years-old blessing. Civetta's parish church is a tiny affair and the crowd has to gather on the street outside once its small chapel is filled. This is the time when emotions begin to surge strongly. One young woman in her early twenties emerged from the blessing with tears coursing down her face; it was a scene I was to witness later through the rest of the day.

The *comparsa*, the appearance of costumed men (never women) marching in the historical parade, left for their departure place outside the Duomo before marching down to Il Campo.

I decided to drift down to Il Campo after the Blessing to get there early enough to secure a place on the inside rail. It was both a good and a bad decision.

The good news was that I did get that railing position, if not near the best part of the track. The bad news was that I then had to endure more than three hours in the piazza in the heat of a searing Tuscan day that turned it into a pizza kiln. Worse, I took only a half-litre of water with me, which quickly turned tepid. A group of two Americans and an Australian on one side of me were even more stupid; they decided to bring bottles of red wine, a decision of sheer folly, I thought. But much to my amazement they seemed to survive the combination of warm wine and hot sun in a relatively unscathed condition.

Almost imperceptibly, the expanse of Il Campo filled. I whiled away the time watching the elite (the ticket-paying rich) in the grandstands on the other side of the track or on the apartment balconies above.

Fortunately in the early evening the sun finally disappeared behind the tall buildings in front of me. The relief was instant and sweet. Just before 5.30, the grand parade began. By this time the centre of Il Campo, inside the track, the grandstands and the balconies above were completely packed. In the centre it was like being in a vast shoal of fish amidst the tens of thousands. I had a shoulder bag with my pathetic bottle of water, notepad and camera; the crowd was so thick it was impossible to put it beside me. I placed it between my legs as some form of security. It was impossible to move more than a few centimetres in any direction. This was a real body-contact sport and reminded me of the hundreds of thousands crammed into the park for the Boston Pops orchestra on Americans' Independence Day. The crowd then was bigger, but the crowd in Siena was far more tightly packed.

And so, like asparagus spears in a can, or the sunflowers in the fields I passed on the drive to the city, we stood bolt upright for the next hour and a half as the parade passed by three times. With the costumes, the trumpets, the flag throwers, the horses, the weapons, it was a spectacular sight.

But, oh, the heat. By the time it finished and all the participants had moved to their own stand in front of the town hall, all I wanted was to get the damned race over and done with.

Like the unnoticed build-up of the crowd, so too had the atmosphere become intense. It was a different intensity of emotion from that of the *prove* in the preceding days. Now there were no songs, no banners being waved (there was no room, anyway). Instead, a nervous tension stalked the crowd. Some laughter here and there, yes. But subdued, almost apologetic for invading the arena. Finally, just before 7 p.m., the horses emerge with their riders from the podesta, the courtyard beside the town hall. They are in their *contrade* colours, helmeted and barebacked. As each emerges to huge cheers into Il Campo, he is handed his *nerbo*, a whip of cement-hard ox sinew, stretched then dried. The *nerbi* are not just ornamental, nor are they just for spurring on their mounts; the jockeys can also put them into service thrashing or blocking their opponents in the coming race. It's that kind of event.

The jockeys make their way slowly up the Casato, the steeply rising slope with its sharp right turn at the top. This will be the last turn the leading jockey will make in the race before the final short dash to the winning line and glory.

But before the race can begin there are still two excruciatingly unbearable issues to be decided. They add an exquisite, even delicious finishing touch to the build-up that has, in fact, been going on since the final Palio last year.

Slowly the jockeys lead their charges to the area just before the *canapi*, the twin lines of starting ropes. One, the actual start line, stretches right across the track. The second, set back far enough for horses to stand between the two, only partly crosses the course.

Only nine *contrade* will be inside the ropes. The last will be behind the second rope. The line-up across the starting line is vital for victory hopes with the first horse having literally the inside running. The last horse, at the rear, is at an obvious disadvantage but does have one thing to help it. Its jockey will actually decide when the race will start; the others must wait and keep a backward eye on him until he starts his dash. Only then will the starting rope be dropped and the race begin.

The starting line-up is drawn by ballot and announced to the crowd. The exuberance, the martial singing, the flags are now forgotten. An incredible quiet falls over Il Campo as if a heavy snow had somehow fallen in the summer heat. The name of each competing *contrade* is announced. You can almost touch the nervous vibrations swirling around the air.

The first horse, the inside runner, drew an enormous cheer from its supporters in the piazza; it had the clear advantage and thus a strong chance for an early and, hopefully, lasting lead to the winning line (the race finishes where it starts, after the three laps). The crowd hushed again for the next draw. More cheers, but by now groans were becoming evident as hopes began to dim of getting a good position in the starting line. By the end of the draw, the cheers were less than half-hearted, more a recognition of defeat by the last *contrada* than a hope for victory; the groans far overpowered the cheers.

One by one, each horse came forward past the back rope and into its allotted position behind the starting rope. At the end, only the starting horse remained.

Almost inevitably it was Civetta, my Owl.

At least the Civetta jockey had the choice of when to start from his position about five metres back (and he could, and did, roam at will while the others were pinned between the ropes). The crowd stilled again in expectation as he waited, walked around, waited again, considered his timing . . . not once, not twice but three times, horses at the starting line backed away. All would then retire back and be called one by one again to their line-up positions. By now, some thirty minutes after the first horses emerged on to the track, the crowd was as edgy as a troop of soldiers waiting in their trenches before going 'over the top' in World War One.

Finally he made his starting dash. The *canape* or front starting rope dropped; the *mossa*, the start, and my first Palio was off. Around the first turn and they passed me, the drumbeats of the hooves. Then came the treacherous San Martino curve. Riders fall, the horses continue—a riderless horse, a *scorso*, can still win. Down past the Palazzo and the stand with the parade participants they galloped, up the slope to Casato, the other right-angle corner. Three laps. About a kilometre. And about seven centuries of tradition.

It's so quick, you can't see it all because of the crowd. An Italian teen beside me is jumping up and down on my feet. I'm looking for Civetta's wine, black and white colours. I don't yell and scream—I haven't earned that right. But my heart is screaming, 'Go Civetta, go.'

We finished about seventh or eighth. It doesn't really matter, because the only winner is the one to cause the mortar to fire to signal the finish. Its thunder-cracker sound has echoed throughout the city all day, signalling the time for a particular event or activities. The pigeons on the rooftops have been scared witless.

The description seems brief. But then the race is brief. Round and round three times. Watching for your colours. Who has fallen? Have you moved up in the field? Can you possibly get into a winning position? The lead, even? And then it's over. It seemed fitting, writing this, to reflect that brevity. For the real essence of the Palio is not the race. The soul of the Palio is the *contrade*; the Palio is just the fire that heats them.

This July, 1999, the white, green and red of Oca, the Goose, triggered the mortar, adding to its proud history as the winner of the greatest number of Palios; eleven since 1945 and matched only by Selva, the Rhinoceros. Civetta lagged dismally behind with only six wins in these years.

As Oca's horse turned into that final straight, the *contradaioli* began to leap the barriers on to the track even before the horse reached the finish line. By the time the jockey could rein in the horse some fifty metres past the line, it was surrounded by hundreds of cheering, chanting, singing and waving Ocaioli. Tears of joy and pent-up emotion gushed from children, men, grandparents. The banner was lowered from its position above the judges' stand to eager Ocaioli hands on the track below and the winners marched triumphantly from Il Campo.

We losers are left to our own devices as Oca parades through the streets to the Collegiate Church of Provenzano (only after the July race; in August the winners will march to the Duomo) to give thanks to God for the victory and then to their own church.

In my two years of closely following the Palio there were five races; in 2000, it was decided by the *contrade* to hold a special third race to celebrate the Millennium.

Civetta either did not compete or did not win any it ran in. Clearly my support was irrelevant. But I had achieved my aim, to experience the Palio. I reflected on the comment of the first person I met as I sought entry to the mystique and the passion of the Palio.

'Even I don't understand it and I'm Italian, from Naples,' said Signora Matteoli in the Palio administration offices.

'It's in their DNA.'

Sesta Parte

La Chiusura

Mangia bene, caca forte e non temer la morte.
Eat well, shit strongly and don't fear death.

—*Tuscan proverb*

Fourteen

Last–but not lost–days and the last Tuscan

OUR last days in Tuscany were busy ones—visiting places we had not until then seen and undertaking the usual round of goodbyes to the friends we had made. It was also a time for reflection on the culture we had been immersed in during our years in this beautiful part of the world.

We were finally able to arrange some days with Luigi and Emma at their lakeside yachting club just north of Rome. As lakes go, Lago Bracciano was not much to shout about—one hundred and sixty metres at it greatest depth, a modest fifty-seven square kilometres in area and just thirty-three kilometres to drive around.

The YCBE (Yacht Club Bracciano Est) reflects the unassuming nature of its namesake lake. Barely one hundred and twenty members ('You have to be invited to join,' said Luigi) for its 7000 square metres of lakefront land and seventy metres wide beach with its rickety old pier. By Italian standards the YCBE was brand new, just twenty-seven years old. There were some twenty permanent caravan sites but most of the membership was by-the-day-only. The day membership was 900,000 lire a year; a caravan site, when one became available, was 2,000,000 lire a year. By Italian standards this was a very good deal.

Most of the membership came from Rome, about thirty to forty kilometres to the south (depending on what part of the sprawling city you live in). The members favoured the Fireball catamarans as their yacht of choice.

It was a very functional, down-to-earth sort of place. Nothing fancy. Cars parked under the trees at the entrance, the old caravans were lined up along one boundary, the trailer yachts were beside the other, and there was a large communal area with a new toilet block. It was rather like the camping grounds at the beach of my childhood. The communal area, set out under wisteria and some mysterious reddish trumpet-shaped flower, was the focus of the whole place. Here the men would sit and chew the fat when they weren't out sailing. At lunchtime or dinner, Mama would arrive with her baskets of table napkins and tablecloths and plastic dishes and bowls of pasta and salad and meats. And so the meal would begin—and continue well into the night. Long after Mama and the kids retired for the night, the men (those with the caravans or their friends, like us, camping beside them) would be drinking wine while they debated the fortunes of the club, politics or football. A continuous procession of food emerged from a rather spartan kitchen with its lonely gas burner on the floor.

On the first night we drove to a nearby lakefront town. The polished cobblestones shone beautifully in the lamplight of the old part. We watched two impeccably dressed teams on the bocce court in the park along the lake's shore. It was one of those many special nights of Italy as lovers of all ages strolled beneath the trees, watched the fishing boats come in or enjoyed a gelato in the cool mid-evening.

For a little quiet lake it was an incredibly noisy place at night: the members talking until all hours; cars and motorbikes coming back from the restaurants and bars of the towns around; dogs yapping and yelping; the dog owners yelling at them to shut up; screech owls screeching and roosters crowing; planes flying into the Italian Air Force base on the other side of the lake; the guy who started sanding the boat hull at 6 a.m.; cats fighting, which inevitably triggered the dogs again . . .

One of the worst noise nuisances was from the singing of the God brigade at the nearby camping ground. We had, unfortunately, timed our visit to coincide with the Papal Youth Rally to celebrate the millennium year.

Two million earnest young of the world descended on Rome and, after the gathering, the surrounding countryside. They poured from tour buses, marched lustily along roads, proudly carried signs of some religious blessing or another, smiled beatifically at bewildered locals and generally made themselves a damned nuisance. Their self-righteousness was overwhelming.

I could accept the earnestness and enthusiasm of these young people. I could share their enjoyment of the beauty of Italy and of life itself. I could wish them well for whatever future was waiting to pounce on them. But I protested their belief that their faith gives them to assume they have the God-given right to disrupt the lives of others. It was not just because of the sleep of ourselves and other holidaymakers they disturbed as they sang at full voice into the early morning hours; they would also descend on a town and bring their religious dialogue into its piazza without invitation or even welcome; the 'heathens' on the street or in the cafés would, I'm sure, have far more appreciated the romance of a soft Italian love song or a hefty dose of jazz.

The millennium year, or Jubilee Year as the church decreed it, was good for business. One account estimates that some twenty-four million visitors and pilgrims journeyed to the Eternal City in Year 2000. Many, like the two million for the Youth Day Mass, came for special events. They included Jubilee gatherings for pizza chefs (they created a special 'papizza' for Pope John Paul, with mozzarella, zucchini, and yellow peppers to match the papal club 'colours' of white and gold), a lunch for the homeless (each of the homeless, bizarrely, was later given a key chain with the Jubilee logo), motorcyclists (2000 of them), the workers (300,000), the families (200,000), the missionaries (100,000), the athletes (80,000), the sick (35,000), the politicians (5000) and the opening of the Holy Door on Christmas Eve, 1999 (1.4 million).

'I'm sure in nine months we're going to see a huge population boom of babies named "Jubilee",' was the somewhat cynical comment of an American expatriate after noting the rather unchaste behaviour of some of the exuberant celebrants.

Some more statistics on the six-day event:

- The Jubilee visitors outnumbered Rome's summertime residents. During the weekend of the event two out of three people in Rome were Jubilee-ists.
- The city (Rome, not Vatican City) spent two hundred and fifty billion lire on the event.
- Five million bottles of water were handed out over the Jubilee's weekend.
- The party-goers generated more than 1,000,000 kilograms of rubbish—three times the amount created by the whole of Rome at the same time the year before.
- There were twenty-five thousand chemical toilets on the Jubilee site just outside Rome.
- Young people from one hundred and sixty countries attended.
- It was the second largest Papal 'event' ever, after the four-million-strong rally at Manila in 1995.
- More than two thousand extra buses and trams were laid on in Rome; they were needed as a record 3.6 million rides were made on public transport in Rome and its region, Lazio, on the Saturday of the rally.

All this in a country where less than one in five women and little more than one in ten men go to Sunday Mass. If 1997 was a vintage year for Tuscan wine, Year 2000 was a big one for the Vatican business.

After skimming across the waters of Lake Bracciano in Luigi and Emma's catamaran, we went underground in Tuscany. And back in time—not to the twenty-seven year history of the YCBE, but the two thousand seven hundred and more years when the mysterious Etruscan society ruled the Tuscan countryside.

Evidence of this ancient people can be found throughout the part of Tuscany we lived in—broken-down ruins of settlements, inscriptions on stone, funeral urns buried with their owner, town or hamlet names with Etruscan origins like Petroio and Sicille.

They were a Bermuda Triangle civilisation. No one yet knows where they came from before reaching Tuscany. They stayed for some centuries and then vanished again under the might of Roman warriors. Just three hundred and thirty words of their vocabulary are known, thirty of those only since 1992 when a legal deed on a slab now known as the 'Tabula Cortonensis' was handed in to Italian authorities by a Calabrian carpenter who claimed he unearthed it at a worksite near Arezzo.

But there was nothing mysterious about their civilisation, although most of what is known of it comes from what few funeral tombs have remained hidden from grave robbers over the two and more millennia since they moved into the hills of southern Tuscany.

They were an extremely sophisticated civilisation, a loose confederation of twelve separate and self-ruling kingdoms called 'lucomonies'. One of the most important was at Chiusi today, a traffic hub with the motorway between Rome and the north on one side and a rail line to the same destinations on the other. It is about thirty kilometres south of Sinalunga.

They were prolific and skilled artists; the black and copper drawings on their plates, bowls and urns are one of the world's most recognisable art forms.

Beneath Chiusi's old town, they built a system of intricate passageways, probably for water and drainage purposes.

And in a belt around the town they excavated large tombs to bury their dead. Until May 2000, only two tombs were open to the public, on the side of the road leading down to Lake Chiusi in the Valdichiana—the Tomb of the Lion (5th century BC) and the Tomb of the Pellegrina (2nd century BC). A third, the Monkey's Tomb (famous for its wall painting of a monkey hanging from a tree) was closed in 1979 because of light and air pollution. But it is now reopened and its rooms are lit by cold lighting that gives an eerie atmosphere as you walk down a central passageway with indented niches for funeral beds or sarcophagi.

Eventually the civilisation was absorbed by Rome to the south but, remarkably, one small remnant of the Etruscans may remain in a tiny, isolated area around the village of Murlo to the southwest of Siena. It was an important Etruscan settlement and, for centuries after the civilisation disappeared from the Tuscan landscape, it was bypassed by trade, invasions, plagues and sieges. So heavily isolated was it, that there is a belief by some experts that the locals still carry Etruscan DNA.

We went back to Florence to see a more modern Tuscan masterpiece that, like Chiusi's Monkey Tomb, had been under the restorers' hands for years. In the same year, 2000, that the Etruscan tomb was once again on view to the public, so too was the imposing bronze statue of Perseus by Benvenuto Cellini. After years of meticulous and expensive restoration, the seven-metre, 1800-kilogram statue was returned to its original abode in the open terrace of Piazza della Signoria's Loggia dei Lanzi.

Fittingly—and no doubt timed to perfection—it was returned on the 500th anniversary of its birth.

Glistening and glittering under the hot midsummer sun, it is a stunning visual scene. There stands Perseus, the son of Zeus and Danae, sword in hand and holding aloft the snake-covered head of Medusa. At his feet lies her body. The green patina of exposure to the pollution of Florence's air (and the assaults of football fans who used it as a climbing platform to celebrate victories) has disappeared, leaving the original bronze and even the gold surface on parts of the statue to glimmer with life and the muscled strength of the victor of good (Perseus) over evil (Medusa).

That it was ever created seems a miracle. Cellini himself tells of the casting in his autobiography. He set the fire to such a high temperature that he got a fever and had to go to bed, leaving behind an assistant.

Then things began to go wrong: the melted bronze began to cool too quickly and his foundry (in his home) caught fire.

Rising from his sickbed, he flung any material on hand into the furnace. Even his own cutlery and the family pewter were not spared. Two days later, the complete figure was revealed. Only three toes were missing; they were 'grafted on' later.

We sought culture of a different type, too. In the hills of southern Chianti, about twenty minutes' drive from Siena, stands the Castello di Brolio.

If Hans Christian Andersen had written about it, he would have undoubtedly depicted it as the abode of a dark knight, a Darth Vader of the Middle Ages—the sort of guy whose idea of fun was a Sunday afternoon of rape and pillage, just to keep his hand in.

It had none of the fairytale beauty of mad Ludwig's Black Forest folly. It lacks the haughty grandeur that imposes itself above the streets of Edinburgh. It lacks even the simple elegance of the rounded corner turrets that grace the modest little 12th century castle of the Cacciaconti family in Trequanda.

Instead, it squats sullenly on its hilltop—a grim, forbidding presence. Even the steep winding road up to its walls is a daunting welcome mat as it passes through tall, pressing conifers. Yet from behind those stern, fifteen-metre-high walls emerged one of the glories of Italy.

For a thousand years it has sat there, the Castello di Brolio. Sieges, sackings, razings and rebuilding . . . it has still survived to achieve its pragmatic purpose of guarding, defending and fighting. Throughout those ten centuries, that millennium, it has done that, mostly successfully.

For nearly nine hundred of those years, successive generations of the noble Ricasoli family have walked its battlements or the graceful ornamental garden below its outer courtyard. From there, they gazed to the towers of Siena on the distant horizon to the west. Behind them, the darkly wooded hills and gullies of Chianti marched to Florence in the north. On their left, these lords and ladies of nobility could even see the high cone of Monte Amiata in the south. And all around them lay the vines and olive groves of their accumulating estates. The original castle, built around 1000 AD, housed a sect of monks. But in 1141, the monks agreed to trade it to the Ricasoli family—a simple exchange of properties. And there the Ricasolis have been ever since.

As the wars between Florence and Siena swirled around the hills and fields of Tuscany, the castle was captured by the Florentines. It was the most southern outpost of Florence—and a daunting one with its view across to Siena. The castle generated a saying: 'When Brolio growls, all Siena trembles.'

For the next few hundred years, those walls faced attacks and sieges from a variety of invaders. But the unity of the Tuscan cities under the grand duchy of Florence brought peace finally to the castle and the Ricasolis could return safely to growing their crops and olives and grapes.

For three hundred years, life carried on serenely; the planting of spring, the growth of summer, the harvest of autumn and the hibernation of winter. Generations of *Barone*, Ricasoli Barons, were born, and died. One, Bettino Ricasoli, was to step from behind the castle walls to make two major marks on Italy's history books.

He was known as the 'Iron Baron', a name that suggests a tyrannical rule. Even the family's own literature recalls him as a man of 'unyielding temperament'. He was also a staunch defender of family values: 'Brolio incarnates the antiquity and nobility of the family.' Well, that was the kind of stuff they wrote back in 1853.

He inherited his title in 1829, when he was only twenty years old. In later years he was to become the newly united Italy's second prime minister.

But it was his knowledge of the wines of Chianti that has left his stamp on us today. There is a Chianti wine and a Chianti region of Tuscany. A Chianti Classico must come from a strictly designated region.

In 1874, after years of testing and researching, he defined the formula for Classico wine. The grape variety mix was precisely laid out in his 'iron rule' letter to a professor at the University of Pisa that year.

'The San Gioveto grape gives the wine most of its aroma and a certain sensory vigour; Canaiuolo adds a sweetness that tempers its austerity without mitigating its aroma; Malvasia, which could be eliminated in wines destined for ageing, softens the first two grapes, adding immediate flavour and making it lighter and ready to drink as a daily wine.'

One hundred and twenty years later, in 1996, new regulations adopting this formula were brought into force for creating Chianti Classico. They also banned the addition of white grapes in the production of the fuller-bodied Chianti wines. The decline of the quality of Chianti in the 1970s and 1980s can probably be attributed to this addition of white grape.

Today's Barone, Francesco Ricasoli, now presides over a 1200-hectare estate, mostly in the Gaiole/Chianti area. The bulk of the hilly land is wooded—oaks, chestnuts, fir and larch. Two hundred and fifty hectares produce the crimson and green rivers of plenty, the wine and the olive oil.

At the end of the 1960s the Ricasoli family sold the wine-making part of the estate to the multinational Seagram company, more noted for the quality of its gin than its wine. The Ricasoli family retained the castle and all its lands.

In what must have been a carefully calculated campaign, the young Barone Francesco bought back the winemaking from the foreign owners in 1993.

'It had lost a lot of money. The concentration was on volume instead of quality,' explained the Barone as we walked through the cellars in the old farm building complex below the brooding castle at the top of the hillside.

'Now I am trying to re-establish the quality.'

He is a slightly-built Barone, almost elfin. And he is the first to admit he has 'no background' in viticulture. In fact, his working career was spent as a photographer in the advertising industry.

When he took control, there were some thirty Ricasoli labels. He has slashed those to just seven, including one *vin santo* dessert wine. Changing the image is a daunting task as the Ricasoli label and name was used by the 'upstart' owners who ran the wine down. That is why he changed the label on his higher market wines to 'Castello di Brolio'.

'That was my philosophy, to reduce the number of labels and instead have a chateau concept.'

Today, the business employs seventy people and is 'probably' the largest estate in the Chianti district's seventy thousand hectares between Siena and Florence—the first area in the world to be defined as a wine producing zone. Although conscious of his notable past—his reclaiming of the family business is testimony to that—the thirty-second Barone di Brolio is not one to linger there.

'If you are only attached to the past, you lose yourself. The past is gone. You have to look forward. That is the only way to keep the business and do it professionally.' He is also keenly aware of the meaning of 'being Tuscan'.

'This is the centre of Italy.' He means not just physically but spiritually.

The Brolio 'Chianti Museum' is a special part of the estate—here, in dim lighting, a bottle of every Chianti produced by the Ricasoli family since the Iron Baron's edict is kept. Barone Francesco's love and knowledge of wine is also evident from his collection in what he calls the 'Library' of other wines from elsewhere in Italy and also France.

In those last days I also had time to get a final haircut from my barber. Mario could have made himself a handy living in the Inquisition, hiring himself out to the church to drag confessions from heretics in the torture chamber.

Not, mercifully, because he threatens me with physical

torment or eternal damnation. Comfortingly, he shows no signs of fiendish ways to make me talk as I sit helpless in his barber's chair in the village of Pozzo della Chiana.

His usefulness during those dire days of terror would have been his skill in wielding the enormous range of instruments that the Inquisition helped devise to rack, skewer, saw and burn faithlessness out of its victims.

The range of implements that Mario requires to trim my modest thatch is truly amazing: old-fashioned straight-razor, three pairs of scissors, three types of comb, battery-driven clippers, hairbrush, hair curler, hand-held dryer . . . With all these at his constant beck and call he scoots around my head at an alarming pace. He shaves my neck. He trims my moustache. He removes those annoyingly long eyebrow hairs that seem to be a part of growing old. He trims the pepper-and-salt growth of my sideburns where I have missed them while shaving. He skims hair fuzz from the top of my ears, then lunges into them to destroy any that have grown since his last attack on my head. Only then does he descend on what I regard as my real hair.

He hasn't got up my nose yet. But I fear that when he discovers tweezers he'll be up there dragging out nasal hairs and whatever might be attached to them.

He is nothing if not thorough—and a rarity in more 'advanced' hair-care countries where barbers are now dressers or stylists, where men and women sit alongside each other gazing into the mirror ahead with awe at the personal secrets of complete strangers, where wine and sherry are offered and where there are more potted plants than a gardening centre.

No such nonsense at my barber's—no plants, no soft pastel décor, no 'ambient and discreet' lighting, no trendy young things flashing fake smiles and eyelashes (his only concession to a helping hand is a tall, thin young man who sweeps out the debris and cleans hair sticking to scissors; he has a long black mane tamed by a ponytail and a wispy goatee beard that he has curiously dyed a straw colour), and certainly no women sitting in his chairs.

But Mario is an excellent barber, not one of those who still believes that the only good haircut is short back and sides. He concedes to modern mores by recognising that that relic of the 1950s is just not wanted by today's young folk. I'm sure, however, that he would oblige if that was what I suddenly decided to have in some nightmare of nostalgia.

He is a thoroughly good-natured man, short and made rather portly from the Italian good life. I was introduced to him by Lassi the Finn after commenting on the excellent haircut he had recently had.

'Oh, I get it done here in Pozzo,' he said.

I was amazed. I had begun to tire of finding a hairdresser who would not cut my waves at their peak so that after the next wash, my hair would be a mass of sticky-up-and-out bits.

We agreed to introduce me the next time he visited the establishment a month or so later. After introductions all round I had my first experience under his hands and implements. It seemed alright and Nancy approved so he became my regular. Later, she would reinforce this. 'You always come back looking five or ten years younger.' Or; 'If you were a woman you'd pay three hundred dollars in Manhattan for all the things he does.' Or, 'Your eyebrows look so good, they're always the first thing I notice when you come back.' My barber had the Nancy seal of approval, the hairdressing equivalent of the Congressional Medal of Honour and Victoria Cross combined. He was also cheap, a bonus.

There is an old Tuscan proverb: '*Chi vuol udir novelle, dal barbier si di con bello,*' 'Who wants to hear short stories, the barber tells them beautifully.' For centuries, the local barber's has not necessarily been the place to go for a haircut, but a meeting place to bring news, gossip, and bemoan the weather and other matters of concern. Mario's is no exception.

So my regular visits always provided some new diversion. One day as I sat waiting in the chair while he took payment from his last customer, a steady stream of old people entered the shop and began gathering by the inside of the door. There was even a woman! Some read the paper that he provides each day, others chatted, no doubt about who had died, who had had a baby, who had bought a new tractor and other vital news of a small community. The barber pointed to an inside door near the entrance. 'Carte,' he said. From this I gathered that this was a regular card-playing school that used a spare room at the barber's to gather and play. By the time I left, the school was still accumulating and numbered a dozen or more. As the crowd had still made no move into the room, I assumed they were waiting for everyone to arrive or perhaps just the person with the key or the cards.

On another occasion, a travelling salesman came into the shop in mid-cut. He had a large poster of some handsome young guy with what was obviously the latest hair design fashion. This he unrolled and hung from his hands for us all to admire. My man rushed to a little cabinet behind me and emerged with a magazine. He opened it and brought it over to me.

'*È migliore, eh?*' he asked. It was a sex magazine and the big-breasted woman with the cutaway bra did, indeed, look better, I had to agree.

Mario was obviously impressed to have me as a customer. He remembers I am from remote New Zealand, a bit like coming from the moon. One afternoon, he asked Lassi where I lived in Tuscany; this was the same day I had myself been in the morning.

'Near Petroio,' said Lassi, 'about half an hour's drive from Pozzo.'

'Ah, think of how many barbers he must pass to get here,' said Mario with flushed pride that someone, a *straniero* to boot, would consider travelling so far to his establishment.

'*Nuova Zelanda*, you could get there by drilling,' added one of the town's old guys who gathers there to gossip, miming a drilling motion at the floor.

He also offers another service from the pages of barbering pre-history—the brush-and-foam, cutthroat-razor *barba* or shave. And a surprising number of his customers avail themselves; they are a regular sight on my visits. One man with a huge walrus moustache borrowed scissors and carefully clipped a little here and a little there in the mirror. I couldn't blame him; it was a handsome piece of art, the product of years of growing, and if I was of a bent towards such a Stalin-like upper lip I would not let anyone else near it.

In my five decades, I had never indulged myself in a cutthroat razor shave, heard the rasp of the deadly blade across my throat or felt the fear of a sudden sneeze. I resolved to experience this ancient art before it becomes totally extinct, like the passing of the dinosaurs, and the crystal radio set.

The boy lathered me up while Mario stropped his cutthroat. Me, I just sat there like the next sheep in line at the meatworks. It was, in fact, completed very quickly and with the skill you had prayed for. Sadly, I must report that modern technology has overtaken the ancient traditional ways—the safety razor I use does a much smoother job. But I was glad to have experienced it.

Cutthroat razors, cards, the men-only gossip centre . . . Mario's little barbershop is an anachronism. But then so are many of the images of this rural land. It was like stepping aboard the *Tardis* for a trip back to 1950s New Zealand when I was just a child. My mother wore slippers and an over-smock to go shopping, just as the Mamas do here. Often she would be in curlers beneath a scarf, an image recreated here. The bicycles with shopping baskets hung from the front handlebars—those big, clumsy, highly unsophisticated ones—are exactly the same that my mother rode, sternly erect because of the stiff-angled seat and its height from the pedals. She too had a wicker shopping basket, just like those you can buy in the Sinalunga market today.

It is a time warp in a country that produces the Ferrari and the Milan fashion houses. Yet Mario, the small village barber, brings an Italian style of his own to his craft, anachronism or not.

On our last night in Tuscany, we said goodbye to Hannalore and Reiner, the Germans who had befriended me from my earliest days and then welcomed Nancy into their home. Later we were both glad and sad that we were able to; just a few months after leaving Italy, we received word that Hannalore—a vibrant, warm, laughing person—had died. We had no details, but presume it was sudden as she was only fifty-eight and there had been no indications, physically or verbally, that something was amiss.

It was Reiner who told us about the curious customs surrounding buying or renting property.

In most countries I'm familiar with, it's a very civilised procedure. The seller or lessor sets a price. It's above what he realistically thinks he'll get but it allows negotiating room. And who knows, some mug may come along and fork out the inflated price. Let's say it's twenty per cent above what he'll accept. The interested buyer or lessee knows what he wants to pay, so comes in with an offer twenty per cent below what he realistically expects to pay but it too allows negotiating room. And who knows, maybe the mug will accept the lower amount.

And so the negotiating begins. Offer and counter-offer. Finally, at about halfway between, after one party comes up twenty per cent and the other party down twenty per cent, the deal is consummated. Everybody's happy. They each knew that midway point was about what the deal was worth but both sides have saved some face.

In Tuscany, the vendor's opening price is just a *starting* price. When the Germans decided to sell their home outside Trequanda and rent an apartment to see if they wanted to stay in Tuscany (they came for one year and stayed seven—it's that kind of a place) or move back to Germany or somewhere else, they found an apartment in an all-but-deserted farm hamlet, isolated away behind hills on the A-road from Siena to Rome (not to be confused with the autostrada toll motorway) and about fifteen kilometres from Trequanda. The asking rental was eight hundred thousand lire a month. Reiner met with the woman and said, yes, he was interested. She said she would have to check with her brother. Lo and behold, the next time they spoke the woman was very sorry but now the price has to be one million lire a month. We heard similar tales from other people.

The lessons are:
- As soon as you show interest, you are fair game.
- Be prepared to have patience, to take your time; some house deals we heard about took a year or more to reach

agreement.

- Be prepared to walk away at any stage—for your sanity if not for your chequebook's sake.

Another example of the rather cavalier attitude of lessors to the tenants came from Crista, the wife of Nancy's Italian teacher, Joe. She rented a ground floor apartment as her art studio on the outer wall of Sinalunga's old town. It was a grim little warren—dimly lit by a few bare light bulbs connected by exposed wiring, bare and unpainted walls, no hot water. But for five hundred thousand lire a month she could live with it. The landlady had also refused to 'lock in' the rental with a signed lease.

One day, the landlady walked in and announced an increase to 1.2 million lire a month. She also wanted a signed lease now. Joe went upstairs to see the family renting the apartment with hot water above. They were paying seven hundred thousand lire a month and had a lease. Crista walked out and bought her own studio.

As far as Joe could determine, the landlady's accountant must have told her she needed so much extra income a month to live. She couldn't charge the upstairs family extra—they were on a lease. So Crista had to be the cash cow.

Later still, poor Reiner was to come up against another confusing custom, '*Chiave a mano*', literally 'key in the hand'. His attempts to find an apartment without constant price jack-ups were a failure. So he decided to buy an apartment and successfully negotiated a price for one sitting right on the outside wall of the old town in Foiano della Chiana. He duly turned up with his deposit at the agreed time—and then owner and buyer sat across the table chatting about nothing in particular. The owner kept shuffling and fiddling with the house keys in his hand.

'I know not what is goes on,' Reiner said.

Making matters worse, Reiner's Italian was not good and he didn't know the protocol, what to do. Finally he took out the deposit cheque and handed it over. The delighted seller quickly passed him the dangling keys and the deal was consummated. The paperwork and contract signing could follow in due course, but at that instant the seller relinquished ownership and Reiner took possession because he now held the keys to the property. All else was mere follow-up legalities. '*Chiave a mano*'—it's a different way of doing business but not necessarily a strange one. It implies trust that the buyer will fulfil his end of the deal, which is a typically Tuscan approach to life and one we could all learn from, foregoing the expense, exchanges of 'important' letters and confusing legalese between overpaid lawyers.

And so our days at San Clemente and in Tuscany came to an end. We left the villa three years to the day after I first arrived. But after those three years, 'progress' in that southern rural area was already changing its character as the march of tourists continued to move south, seeking a more peaceful and simple holiday environment.

The number of tourists had probably doubled in Trequanda over those years. So too had the range of languages and accents. Car numberplates from much further afield also reflected this growth. Giorgio had a snazzy new sign up outside his Bar Paradiso and *gelateria*; he had also opened a pizzeria inside. Cariplo, the pension fund that owned the farmland around San Clemente and more on the road from Trequanda to Sinalunga, had begun construction of a big new apartment complex on the hill above its wine-bottling plant. At Bagno Vignoni, construction had begun on what looked fated to be a tacky set of pools for footbathing. We wouldn't be surprised if they installed a water park with slides for the kids. The simple charm of sitting on the dirt bank with your feet in the overflow trench from the spa pool in the town's central piazza would be unlikely to survive this modernity for many more years.

Our last Tuscan was Moro, Sinalunga's town drunk. He starts his morning at Giorgio's bar that fronts on to the station platform. By 10.30 he is pretty well oiled and ready to regale you with the services he provided to the advancing Allies when they set up a base here before moving further north during the war. His English is very fractured and one can only assume his services did not include translation; he would probably have lost the war for the Allies single-handed. With his drugstore-bought teeth and his blood alcohol level, his Italian is pretty unintelligible, too.

After his early morning libation, he hops aboard his little motor scooter and winds his way up the steep hill opposite the station piazza to the old town where he teams up with his chums, moving between the two bars on opposite sides of the Piazza Garibaldi to chew the fat with the other old guys who gather at them each day. Another few wines and its back down the hill to Mama, lunch and a siesta.

He first discovered me as he emerged from the station bar one morning as I walked to my bank. *Stranieri* are easy to pick out and he targeted me.

'*Inglese?*' he asked me.

'*No, Nuova Zelandese.*'

'Ah, *Nuova Zelanda*. In *La Guerra*, the war, when Allies are here I meet many—*Inglesi, Sudafricani, Australiani, Neozelandesi*. I help them.'

And that was to be his basic topic of conversation in the coming years. At first I found him to be a pain in the arse, even more so when he first met Nancy after she arrived.

'Just humour him and we'll try to get away as quickly as possible,' I warned her as he pounced on my new wife with the same story.

It was completely the wrong way to deal with him, as we were to learn later. Trying to escape merely encouraged him to hang onto your arm and continue to talk in his mix of drunken Italian and dreadful English (to be fair, my Italian was as bad as his English). Treating him like a pest only encouraged him to be one. But if you just smiled and let him have his say, he would be quite content and drift away after a moment's brief greetings.

In this way, we came to realise and appreciate his many fine qualities—his warm eyes and smile, his generosity, his genuineness, his delight to practise his few remaining words of English on the *stranieri*.

He also took a shine to Nancy and she always received a

special greeting from him. Sometimes he would disappear into the bar and emerge with a small sweet for her (and he always felt obliged to buy one for me, too). In return, we would buy him the occasional glass of *vino*. Over time we forged a casual but fond relationship with Moro.

And there he was on the platform of Sinalunga station as we waited for the Siena train to take us to Chiusi for our connection to Rome. As ever he was unshaven with his few white wisps of hair hopelessly dishevelled and his rumpled old clothes demonstrating again that he was not one to give concessions to the notion of sartorial elegance, this short little Tuscan with his face ravaged by alcohol and the climate. He emerged, typically, with glass of wine in one hand and a *focaccia* sandwich in the other. His face beamed with pleasure then confusion as he noticed our suitcases. He was genuinely crestfallen when we told him, yes, we were leaving, yes, and Italy, and yes, for good. It was about 1 p.m. and the reason he had overstayed his usual 'visiting hours' at Giorgio's bar was that he was waiting to say goodbye to his daughter who had been visiting him and his wife. Or perhaps he had been earlier, made his rounds up town and then come back for the farewells.

He disappeared into the bar and returned with a bag containing several *focacce* that he gave us. 'For the travels, for *il treno* (the train).' It was a kind gesture.

After a string of laments and sorrows, he suddenly astounded us by bursting into song, The Platters' 'Only You'. In perfect English! One hand on his heart and the other on Nancy's shoulder, he proceeded through at least the first verse. He was obviously quite caught up with the emotion of it all.

As the train pulled in we scrambled to get our luggage up the narrow entrance steps to a carriage. The Italian railways system is no hostage to its customers; a train stop lasts one minute and if you're on, fine, if not, there'll be another one. The carriages are also atrociously awkward for travellers with suitcases and other luggage. None of the entranceways are flush with the platform so you have to heave yourself and your luggage up a narrow stepwell of five or six steps. On a major route such as Milan-Bologna-Florence-Rome-Naples, with millions of Italian travellers and foreign tourists a year, it is a callously offhand treatment of those fare-paying passengers. At the time we left, a new separate terminal and coaches had been built for the Roma Termini–Leonardo da Vinci airport run of about thirty minutes. Here, you would have thought, was an ideal opportunity to demonstrate at least some lip service to customer convenience: a high-profile train run, millions of visitors from around the world, a flash new platform and carriages. Here was the chance to have wide doorways flush to the platform with plenty of storage space for luggage. But no, the concept proved too overwhelming for management and it was the same old scramble up the narrow stepwell and do what you like with the luggage that won't fit in the overhead racks (which were only wide enough to take hand luggage anyway, certainly not large suitcases).

So we scrambled aboard, dumped most of our gear in the little doorway area and sat down. As the train moved out of the station, there was Moro, his arm raised in farewell (wine glass in his left hand).

The words of his song seemed to follow us out on our journey to Chiusi, particularly the bit about making dreams come true.

On our right, the hills called *i monti* on whose slope we had spent those years; past l'Amorosa, the beautiful old farmhouse complex where we had such a memorable lunch; through Torrita di Siena, home of the annual donkey race and blues festival; high on its hilltop, Montepulciano, home of *vino nobile*, the Renaissance church San Biagio and the annual *bravio delle botti*, barrel race. On the left, the flat plain of the Valdichiana with its backdrop of the Italian spine, the Apennine mountains.

Ciao Toscana.

We left with the sadness of saying goodbye to great friends and beautiful countryside and a warm-hearted people. But we had no real regrets. It was time to move on, to experience new places.

If only we knew where that might be.

Also by Penguin New Zealand

Seasons in Tuscany

Allan Parker

Two chance encounters during one beautiful English summer led
New Zealander Allan Parker into a lifestyle that many of us can only
dream about: he was offered a house-sit in a 300-year-old villa in
Tuscany and he fell deeply, passionately in love with Nancy.

Seasons in Tuscany is the story of these two loves. The day-to-day
goings-on in a small Italian town are captured with warmth and
humour: from feast days to food festivals, from market days to grape
harvests – this is the life.

Over 12,000 copies sold